Invisible Fight

Discover the Hidden Battlegrounds of the Heart
and How to Remain Established in Jesus

JACKY ELWOOD

Published by Author Academy Elite
PO Box 43, Powell, OH 43065
AuthorAcademyElite.com

Identifiers:
Library of Congress Control Number: 2021902573
ISBN: 978-1-64746-717-3 (paperback)
ISBN: 978-1-64746-718-0 (ebook)

Available in paperback and e-book

Scripture quotations taken from the Amplified® Bible (AMPC), Copyright © 1954, 1958, 1962, 1964, 1965, 1987 by The Lockman Foundation Used by permission. www.Lockman.org

Scripture quotations are from the ESV® Bible (The Holy Bible, English Standard Version®), copyright © 2001 by Crossway, a publishing ministry of Good News Publishers. Used by permission. All rights reserved.

Scripture taken from the New King James Version®. Copyright © 1982 by Thomas Nelson. Used by permission. All rights reserved.

Scripture quotations marked (NLT) are taken from the Holy Bible, New Living Translation, copyright ©1996, 2004, 2015 by Tyndale House Foundation. Used by permission of Tyndale House Publishers, a Division of Tyndale House Ministries, Carol Stream, Illinois 60188. All rights reserved.

Any Internet addresses (websites, blogs, etc.) and telephone numbers printed in this book are offered as a resource. They are not intended in any way to be or imply an endorsement by Author Academy Elite, nor does Author Academy Elite vouch for the content of these sites and numbers for the life of this book.

Dedication

To everyone with whom I have crossed paths in life. I'm honored to have met you, and I pray my life reflected the love that Jesus Christ has shown to me. May we all *"seize and hold tightly the confession of our hope without wavering, for He who promised is reliable and trustworthy and faithful [to His word]"* (Hebrews 10:23, AMP).

Contents

Part 1
The Hidden Dilemma

Part 2
Blessed Assurance

Part 3
Established

Acknowledgments

I am deeply grateful for all those who have encouraged me through this writing project, especially my husband Jason and my beta readers who took the time to do the first read through. Liz, Michaela, Alaina, Anne, Joan and Jess, thank you for pushing me to see things more clearly so I could write better. I am also thankful to Author Academy Elite for paving the way for people like me to serve others through writing.

Introduction

We live in a world that says, in many ways, "If you just make a good impression, that's all that matters." But you will never be a man or woman of God if that's your philosophy. Never. You can't fake it with the Almighty. He is not impressed with externals. He always focuses on the inward qualities, like the character of the heart ... those things that take time and discipline to cultivate.

—Pastor Chuck Swindoll

I don't know about this place, I thought while sitting across from a gym manager, contemplating a future membership. Gyms make me a little uneasy, but this was my best option. I was newly married and wanted to stay active and healthy, so finding the right gym was crucial for keeping me motivated. The manager was nice—a little over zealous—but I guess that was needed to sell memberships. As he guided me around his tiny gym hidden in a downtown strip-mall, I remember thinking it was a little dated with zigzag stripes on the wall.

But I wondered if everything else was up to date. Walking through each section, the manager made every inch seem awesome. His exuberance grew as he explained each machine and the amenities included with a membership. "Check out our step ladders and TV screens on the bikes. Oh, and by the way, your first personal training session is free!"

Uh, what? Who said anything about a trainer? I wondered in my head. Yeah I was a little defensive, but I politely acknowledged I would think about it. We pressed on. As the tour wrapped up, all I thought was *this seems like it has everything I need, but how do I know what's really being promised?* Back then, there wasn't a one-week free-trial option, so I had to chance it.

After thinking about it, and without other options nearby, I jumped in, signing up for a year. Sad to say, within a month or two, I realized the impression first given had masked broken equipment and an unwelcoming staff who made me uncomfortable. I thought, *Great, a year of this with no out, except if I paid a hefty fine.* Also, the free training session? Don't ask me why, but I took the offer. This made the situation even worse—a misleading experience wasting my membership— since I never returned afterward.

Impressions are how we make decisions. How we gauge if we have trouble or not. It's our first glance beyond the exterior without knowing what the inside situation will be. Everyone makes a first impression, but are the impressions tainted by a messy interior? Just as the gym was tainted with invisible brokenness and disappointment, our hearts can be hiding the exact same things. The reflection we offer to the world tells us what's happening deep within, even when we might not recognize these hidden facets ourselves. To be a person who is the same on the outside as the inside takes a mindset that understands and remembers how quickly the external withers, while it is also joyous that the internal will stand forever.[1]

We have all faced people or experiences that turned out different than what we thought or hoped:

- A job that was not what we hoped

- A relationship that was not what we imagined

- A church that was not what we believed

- An experience where expectation was undesirable

Disappointment is painful. When the heart gets burned, it's difficult to look past all the debris and actually see what we need to see. It's not hard to grow calloused in the process.

We all have a chance to recognize the broken parts and allow the Lord to make us whole again. When we allow Him in, He will allow us to see more clearly and find the joy that has been there all along. Romans 15:13 says, *"May the God of hope fill you with all joy and peace in believing, so that by the power of the Holy Spirit you may abound in hope" (ESV).*

Jon Bloom wrote, "Our hearts were never designed to be followed, but to be led. Our hearts were never designed to be gods in whom we believe; they were designed to believe in God."[2]

The heart—the inner core to our character and integrity—is in constant tension. The tension can be brutal, which is why we must keep fighting, refining, and recognizing when our hearts may have some blockage. The *invisible fight* is real; the tensions no one else sees can damage or be fatal if we aren't careful. The good news is transformation is always available, but we must allow truth to sink in and stick. We can't have a healthy life without being established in the Lord first. To be sustained, upheld, steadfast, fixed, and firm on the right principles means we are established in and trust the Lord.[3] It means once we accept by faith the gift given by Christ, our renewed hearts can do what they were meant to do.

In a world where people only want to see the outside and think they are doing ok, I pray we yearn to look inside and say we can do better. We want to see Him better. We recognize our faults and sins for what they are, and we learn to become disciplined and steadfast in the Lord. It's through this deeper look that we can recognize the hidden battle grounds of the heart and lean into God's promises, no matter what. The Lord is the One who allows the heart to be led toward established holiness. Yet we must be willing to change and know we gain freedom in Him. Weaknesses can be hidden and, when not managed, will overflow in built-up callousness. To tackle these weaknesses, we must allow the Lord to strengthen our new hearts so we can enter each season with purpose. The seasons may be hard, but they mature us, refine us, restore us, and continue to bring opportunities to bear fruit. One foot in front of the other is all it takes; little steps matter because we are moving forward.

I'm honored you found this book. My heart is not to tell stories or give an opinion but to encourage through stories and shared truth from God's Word. We all face hardship, discouragement, fear, and pain that dig in deep. However, we have the ability to regain focus and experience true transformation. We can have a wholeness in Christ that leads to holiness, a renewed reverence for the One who created our hearts from the beginning. Things shared here may not be new, or maybe they are. All I pray is the Lord will show His love in a whole new way through this book, through His Word, and allow everything else to flow over us, if needed. I pray this is an encouragement, and hope will be experienced in the future. Our race isn't over, and there's plenty more fight left to give. *The invisible fight* takes time and discipline to cultivate. We've got this—so, let's keep going!

PART 1

The Hidden Dilemma

CHAPTER 1

Don't Want to Go There: Calloused Hearts

Make up your mind God; is it yes or is it no?
Yes, that's how I talk to Him whenever my heart is not in the right place. Since elementary school, I loved to sing, my passion grew as I got older, and I realized I wanted to follow Jesus for the rest of my life. *A worship leader is what I'll be!* It seemed clear this was the direction I should go as the passion grew in my heart. But sometimes, God says, "I want you to go in another direction."

For years, I sang on a worship team. Heck, that's where I met my husband! This was exactly what I wanted to do, but after all these years, why did it seem as if God closed the door for good? If I'm being honest, I was fine with the change, at first saying to myself, *God knows best, and I trust Him.* But deep down, the disappointment would overwhelm me. The lies would creep in, saying, *I'm not good enough* and *will never be good enough.* I believed them. There were real moments

3

I felt inadequate, and that feeling spread into everything I did. My passion, my dream for the Lord was being trampled and squashed. There were times I became bitter and critical, especially about other worship leaders—or down right mad about being unable to use my gifts. The desire in my heart was not being met, and I started doubting the goodness of God. I had an attitude that if God wasn't going to allow me to do what I wanted, giving up would be the best option. My mind bullied me into thinking my failures meant my giftings didn't matter. Idleness took root and caused me to limit God and myself. I created a callousness that infected my heart.

Round And Round We Go

For many of us, myself included, emotion and reason dictate our lives instead of listening to the Word of God. Round and round we go, demanding God show His signs and wonders in our lives so we can keep moving forward and believe in Him. All the while, He is repeating, "You're going the wrong way. All I want is for you to know my ways above all else." God wants everything to count, but we need to believe in His promises and fully trust Him—instead of blaming Him.

In the Bible, we see the Israelites grumble and complain all the time. The blame game was their love language of choice. As a result, they would wander in the wilderness, never to enter the land God had promised. Exodus 17: 1–7 (ESV) says:

> *All the congregation of the people of Israel moved on from the wilderness of Sin by stages, according to the commandment of the Lord, and camped at Rephidim, but there was no water for the people to drink. Therefore the people quarreled with Moses and said, "Give us water to drink." And Moses said to them, "Why do you quarrel with me? Why do you test the Lord?" But the people thirsted there for water, and the people grumbled against Moses and said, "Why did*

you bring us up out of Egypt, to kill us and our children and our livestock with thirst?" So Moses cried to the Lord, "What shall I do with these people? They are almost ready to stone me." And the Lord said to Moses, "Pass on before the people, taking with you some of the elders of Israel, and take in your hand the staff with which you struck the Nile, and go. Behold, I will stand before you there on the rock at Horeb, and you shall strike the rock, and water shall come out of it, and the people will drink." And Moses did so, in the sight of the elders of Israel. And he called the name of the place Massah and Meribah, because of the quarreling of the people of Israel, and because they tested the Lord by saying, "Is the Lord among us or not?"

Oh, the poor Israelites, but can't we all relate to them? As believers, we have God's Word; we read and believe, by faith, what He has done. Yet we still question His plan for our future, especially His plan for our individual lives. We get tangled by confusion, complaining that life isn't going the way we hoped. *Why do we do this?* The Israelites were in God's will, yet they chose not to use His promises or find how powerful they could be in the Lord. They buckled. Instead of running into the situation, knowing God had already foreseen the outcome, they missed the planned promise. They allowed their hard hearts to rule how they responded. With grumbling and complaining, they wished for the past or what had been. A past we all scratch our heads over, wondering *why* they would long to return to such suffering again. We can't buckle as the Israelites.

After the hard reality of not becoming a worship leader, I realized something. I needed to humble myself and experience closed doors to understand obedience better. My desire to serve the Lord as a worship leader got in the way of knowing Him. I think, to some degree, my want and passion ruled me. What *I* needed was not to become a worship leader. What

I needed was a renewed desire for Jesus. I had to fully surrender and trust His plans for my life. Rest in faith that He knows my highest calling. After all these years, many tears, and frustrations, a wonderful thing happened. God opened a new door that led me to write this book. Only He knew my deepest desire buried in my heart and finally wanted me to see it. Not only did He reveal something greater, but He also graciously revealed the sin I needed to uproot.

"X" Marks The Spot

Whenever I see the word callous, I always think of the medical term callus. Both words are defined as a hardness or thickness. Callous is being made hard—hardened—while the medical term callus is a localized, firm thickening of the skin as from repetitive friction. I think of these definitions and am reminded of when I played sports growing up. Oftentimes, painful calluses would appear, mainly on my big toes. The thickened layers created a hard area that caused problems the longer I played and ignored the issue. My feet needed to be soaked, filed, and moisturized when I played sports. *I know—kind of gross. But hey, doesn't this make me a hard-core athlete?* I kid. Because the constant friction of rubbing caused this issue, it could not be ignored for long. This same concept applies to our hearts. The tension is there, this hidden and visible pain, and the longer we go without tending to the issue, the worse it will become. Our callousness needs to be treated. It needs to be recognized, and refined over and over until the thickness is removed.

Any heart not willing to change, forgive, or see its own sin will create a heart that is calloused toward life, God, and others. It's so easy to excuse the subtle hardness in our hearts and miss good things right in front of us. The deceitfulness of sin causes our hearts to struggle, groaning for restoration. The Bible says in Jeremiah 17:9 (AMP), *"The heart is deceitful above all things And it is extremely sick; Who can understand it fully and know its secret motives?"* Because sin lies to us, it makes us believe there isn't a problem. We can tend to brush it off, not letting sin fully bother us as it should. Serious heart issues, like the following, can keep us from moving forward:

- Bitterness

- Jealousy

- Anger

- Unforgiveness

- Pride

- Social Distraction

- A self-absorbed attitude

These issues create voids in our lives that allow sin to creep in, leaving us with debris and nothing to clean it up—or so we believe. We can remove the garbage and rid this callousness by recognizing our hearts are in trouble. We do this by asking the Lord to show us what we have missed. What's really happening with our hearts? Where do we need relief from all the despair?

A simple mosquito bite.

Most likely, we have all endured one of those. They either arrive en masse to devour our bodies or, we were lucky enough, for one bite. Either way, we are left with welts that fester and itch like crazy. I know whenever I'm bitten alive by these critters, the compulsion to scratch usually arrives full force and often while I'm asleep. The next morning, I wake up to a worse situation. My skin is raw, swollen, and bleeding, which means more time needed to heal. What should I do? The scratching frenzy which left my skin in despair probably could have been avoided if I'd only marked the spots with an "X" or used some ointment to prevent the itching.

This got me thinking about sin. How easily it grows or spreads, causing us more pain and brokenness, and it extends our healing. Sin is like that mosquito bite springing up to itch like crazy, begging for instant relief. *Do we give in?* Are we spiritually asleep, not recognizing the scratching? The temptation can become unbearable, but putting an "X" through it, like the ointment, we declare no to that desire and yes to victory. We have the ability and the power to say, no, sin doesn't hold us. Sure, it is hard to resist everything, and our desires won't vanish right away, but we don't have to take it a step further. The result of scratching—the sin—should bother us more than its temporary annoyance. Sin has consequences if we can't control our flesh. That is why we need our hearts to be awake and on guard. We should confidently say we can resist the itch and allow healing instead.

If we want the hardness to be removed, we ask the Lord to reveal the debris, then guard our hearts. Remember what a fleshly outcome could entail. We focus on change. The removing of the dross takes time, but with each layer removed, we notice the following:

- *Bitterness turns into joy:* We begin to let go of our own desires and find completeness in Christ, thanking Him for all He has done.

- *Jealousy turns into encouragement:* We turn what *we should* have into celebrating what God *has given* others.

- *Anger turns into gentleness:* We release our anger into the Lord's hands. We ask Him to open our eyes to negative emotions that are unacceptable and allow His perfect restoration help us live in the wholeness He has for us.

- *Unforgiveness turns into forgiveness:* We know it takes time, and pains may never be forgotten, but we forgive so healing can take place.

- *Pride turns into humility:* We see ourselves in a healthier way. Not as better than the other but as one who knows their place among many.

- *A self-absorbed attitude turns back to Jesus:* We remember who is on the throne in our hearts and lives and allow Jesus to take His rightful place.

Instead of small acts of disobedience, we take small acts of faith, marking the spots of sin early before the situation grows worse. We draw closer to Jesus as we retreat from sin because we understand He's the only One who can help when we are weak. We only need to see and believe.

So Close Yet So Far

The disciples who walked with Jesus daily struggled with heart issues too. The feeding of the 5,000 was another example of how we miss what God wants us to see, and how our hearts can grow calloused. Mark 6: 34–36 (AMP) says:

> *When Jesus went ashore, He saw a large crowd [waiting], and He was moved with compassion for them because they were like sheep without a shepherd [lacking guidance]; and He began to teach them many things. When the day was nearly gone, His disciples came to Him and said, "This is an isolated place, and it is already late; send the crowds away so that they may go into the surrounding countryside and villages and buy themselves something to eat."*

After a long day, the disciples wanted to quickly dismiss the people and not deal with them, but the Lord in his mercy told them to figure it out. Mark 6:37 (AMP) goes on to say, *"You give them something to eat."* As the disciples searched the crowd, looking for food, a little boy's lunch became the handful that would feed thousands. It was with one little boy's two fish and five loaves that sparked a miracle to be witnessed so the Lord could provide enough for all the people to eat. The disciples needed to look past their own desires and really see what God was trying to do. He was leading them to know more of who He was. The sad thing was, they still didn't understand. You would think that while picking up the twelve baskets of leftover scraps, they would be celebrating, or crying joyfully over the miraculous provision that had occurred, but they didn't. They missed it. Their hearts were calloused toward what had happened, and until a storm emerged, the disciples hadn't learned the valuable lesson about their hardened hearts. [4]

Like the disciples, it is easy to forget the good the Lord has promised and done in our lives. We tend to offer mediocre responses like the following:

- Wanting to dismiss people from our lives due to inconvenience.

- Wanting to stay comfortable and not stretch our faith in a manner that would please the Lord.

- Having a victim mentality. The "what's in it for me" mentality can catch us inside a web of selfish thinking and blame the world as the problem, not ourselves or our behavior.

- Being too busy, which creates a lack of community and a loss of love for people.

- Not having or wanting faith in confusing times. It's a choice we have to make. Will we miss what Jesus is trying to teach us because we are too callous.

There are many ways we miss Jesus and His miracles that happen daily. Indifference comes when we become overwhelmed by the tensions instead of the power and deity of Jesus. At times, my lack of hospitality and service have caused friction and a hardness in my heart. My heart would forget how to love and serve in a way that reflects Christ. When a friend needs a favor, a coworker needs someone to listen, a random, lonely stranger needs a helping hand, these are the opportunities to see God work. To magnify Jesus. My first response was sometimes not pleasant. I missed what Jesus tried to teach me, just like the disciples. Let's not become so indifferent we miss the miracles happening right in front of our eyes.

Forward Motion

Hardness of the heart is a choice. Looking back at the Israelites, we see the writer of Hebrews quotes the writer of Psalms, stating this very thing in Psalm 95:8 (AMP). *"Do not harden your hearts and become spiritually dull as at Meribah [the place of strife], And as at Massah [the place of testing] in the wilderness."* Because we have a choice, two things can happen. We either move forward or stay the same. Let's not be like the first generation of Israelites who allowed unbelief to create their hardness of heart. They failed to believe God's promises and retreated to the old heart and ways, dwelling on the past, wishing for its return—or that change had never happened. A new heart knows God, and He can use our past to mold us into the person we are created to be.

Coming from a broken home, I know about messy, complicated, not-so-nice experiences. I've dealt with anger, unforgiveness, and trust issues that run deep. Sure, I could have stayed in that cycle, but healing was waiting for me. To move forward, I had to forgive. I had to let go and pray from my heart. It takes time and is painful, but to have restoration granted to an aching heart is what propels us all.

Life is a constant struggle of being aware when our desires interfere with how God wants to use us. It's hard to look beyond our wants or wishes, but we see God is deeply concerned for us. He is good and works everything out for those who love Him.[5] All it takes is one layer of hardness—one thing that we hold so tightly, to be removed. In removing it, we bring renewing to our souls. There might be uneasiness, that gently prods us onward. Don't ignore it! That gentle nudge is the Spirit, who says, "not that way, but this way" and is guiding us toward purpose and hope. Getting to the heart of the issue is never easy, but is worth it.

CHAPTER 2

One Foot In, One Foot Out: Divided Hearts

From the very beginning, men and women have struggled with the issue of a divided heart. Robert Robinson knew this battle-ground well. A hymn he wrote in 1758 reflects the struggle we often feel today. "Prone to wander, Lord, I feel it; prone to leave the God I love; Here's my heart, Lord, take and seal it; seal it for thy courts above."[6]

The constant tension between the love we have for the Lord and the love we have for the world is never ending. The flesh fights for what it wants, while the Lord fights for our whole hearts. When we lack commitment—to God, His Word, and what He wants for each of our lives—emptiness appears, and our hearts become frozen, unwilling to surrender completely. The one-foot-in, one-foot-out approach cripples us from being free in Christ, allowing sin to weasel its way inside our hearts. As a result, we shrug it off or become buried in shame and guilt that we are numb, idle, never fully surrendering or going all-in with the Lord.

Fickle And Fragile

In many areas of life, there can be an unwillingness to commit to the high moral demands of Christ. We are fragile. We sway, we get confused, and in the midst, we try to go down many roads at the same time. Sometimes, we can't say as it says in Psalm 86:11 (ESV), *"Teach me your way, O Lord that I may walk in your truth; unite my heart to fear your name."* If Jesus is Lord of all in our lives, can we stop? Can we stop doing everything we know we shouldn't? In the midst of this battle, we try to hold on to Christ but allow our hearts to bend to culture. We say, "I have tried", "I have prayed", "I have wept for change", but we can't let go of what's holding us back. Divided hearts can take many forms and are usually a result of compromise and the sin we allowed in our lives. Often, we know there is something missing, but we don't want to let go of the things that distract or sway us. Divided hearts that hesitate to open and commit to God, will cost us and may even jeopardize our lives.

- A TV show or movie we shouldn't watch, yet we do anyway
- An extra snack or drive-thru splurge that makes us feel guilty or throws us off course yet we indulge anyway
- An extra purchase we shouldn't buy and should be saving or blessing others but purchase anyway
- A relationship or friendship we know is wrong or unhealthy but won't end
- Complacency
- Boredom and procrastination

• One more drink; one more fun, crazy experience

The list goes on and on.

Putting ourselves in situations we know lead to compromise only enhances how Satan deceives us. Satan allows us to believe we need these things to be fulfilled to have peace and comfort. This is such a lie. When we buy into these desires, we put ourselves above God and make ourselves the ruler. When we allow this, eventually, we will fall.

Yet we have a choice. Do we want a life walking wholeheartedly with Jesus? Or do we walk away grieved?

Don't Leave Grieved

Throughout the gospels, we see the story of the rich young man: this wealthy, young, influential man came running to Jesus. Why? He knew something was missing in his life and was eager to know how to change. He respected Jesus and wanted to know how he could obtain eternal life. But, we see his heart is not willing to give 100%.

Mark 10: 20–22 (AMP) says:

> *"Teacher, I have [carefully] kept all these [commandments] since my youth." Looking at him, Jesus felt a love (high regard, compassion) for him, and He said to him, "You lack one thing: go and sell all your property and give [the money] to the poor, and you will have [abundant] treasure in heaven; and come, follow Me [becoming My disciple, believing and trusting in Me and walking the same path of life that I walk]." But the man was saddened at Jesus' words, and he left grieving, because he owned much property and had many possessions [which he treasured more than his relationship with God].*

The man thought he was good enough to achieve eternal life. He believed if he followed the rules in this earthly life and was a good person, that was enough. He wanted both riches and eternal life, but God knew his true devotion. God asked him to give his riches up so he could have eternal life instead. The man, however, couldn't do it and walked away grieved. We hope the rich young man did eventually come back and give up everything God asked, but we only have what the Word says. It's sad to see that his heart held him back from experiencing the true freedom in Christ.

To some extent, we have acted like the rich young man. We have divided loyalties. I think we can say this is currently, or was true, at some point. We live a double-minded life with a divided heart, searching for what can complete us. Some would probably say, "I'm mostly happy the way I am, and I don't feel rising tension when it comes to feeling divided." Some may also say, "I try to be nice, compassionate, and do my part, so why should I take the time to care so much?" We can look at the Israelites again for another example on what not to do—how their divided, complacent hearts got in the way. Jeremiah 2:13 (AMP) says:

> "*For My people have committed two evils: They have abandoned (rejected) Me, The fountain of living water, And they have carved out their own cisterns, broken cisterns that cannot hold water.*"

In this passage, Israel committed two sins: forsaking God and replacing the true God with idols. Instead of relying on the refreshing, dependable, consistent, satisfying source, they turned to unpleasant, distasteful, broken-down wells that couldn't hold anything. Abandoning Living Water for broken cisterns was the compromise of choice. To some extent, we mimic a lot of what they did but only secretly. There's a reason God told us about the Israelite's shortcomings—so we would know what a divided heart looks and acts like and the cost it reveals. I guess we should all ask ourselves these questions again. Do we have divided loyalties? What else is captivating our hearts other than Jesus?

Satan's Trap

We all have moments in life when we need to make a decision. Whether it comes to what we want versus what God commands—do we flinch? Do we cave to a callous response and turn away, indulging in mindless gratification? I can't tell you the times I have allowed compromise to fill the void in my divided heart. Food, shopping, TV—these are my weaknesses, my triggers to have a mind consumed by things, while my heart yearns to be filled. When I am not guarded, these lead me on a downward spiral slamming me against guilt and shame every time. In all three areas, I have flinched. But for now, I'll only point to one: television.

Too often we compromise what we put inside our brains and what we allow our eyes to see. Now, before you think I'm being judgy about Netflix, I just want to admit that I was a TV junkie! I loved, breathed, and thought I was living in it. At one point, I was watching twenty different shows regularly. It was like having a second job—sitting and staring at my television while eating constantly. Sad, right?

This was the first thing I had to cut from my life. Not completely, but I am more selective in what I see or spend my time on. It's crazy how a show knows exactly how to reach out, how to pull you in and make you feel like part of a family. How do we get so wrapped up in the characters' lives? When the show ends, why do we feel like a little piece of us has died too? We think about it for weeks, wondering why we feel anxious, sad— never wanting the story to end. That was me. I know I'm not the only one to feel like this either. I mean, not being able to watch new episodes of *The Office,* with Pam and Jim's perfect love story, made my heart shatter—which is beside the point.

In all seriousness, I realized my heart was off course. It had been drifting for a long time. I remember when I first got married and transitioned from graduating to finding a job. I had a lot of time on my hands. The sad thing was, I would spend eight hours or more on my couch. My husband would come home and I would still be watching shows—sometimes without acknowledging him. My limp wave, avoiding eye contact, was selfishness on display, and my husband was its victim. Eventually, I had to ask myself, *Why am I doing this*? Could these shows know how to activate my heart's desires? Did these shows give me satisfaction? Maybe, for a little while, but after a few years, the satisfaction disappeared, never bringing the peace, rest, or joy my heart craved. I was blinded by a fake peace that took years to recognize and identify my boredom with Christ. Yup, I said it. While I'm not proud to admit it, I didn't want to read my Bible because it wasn't entertaining me. In his book, *Competing Spectacles*, Tony Reinke expresses boredom with Christ as the biggest concern in this media age. "In the digital age, monotony with Christ is the chief warning signal to alert us that the spectacles of this world are suffocating our hearts from the supreme spectacle of the universe."[7] The momentary gain from TV sucked me in, giving me exactly what I wanted—to immerse myself in mindless entertainment because I didn't want to deal with my real emotions. I wanted only the good feelings. What I wanted to be real never gave me the same satisfaction as what I knew was real. Yet I wasn't willing to give it up. However, that is exactly what Christ asked me to do. As I was being sucked in emotionally, I would still feel the pull to return to reality.

The test was placed before me countless times, and countless times, I failed. Satan knew exactly how to tempt me. He wanted me to abandon the Word and make it seem boring. Tony goes on to say, "Soul boredom is a great threat, and when our souls become bored, we make peace with sin."[8] I could not make peace with sin any longer—allowing TV to become an idol. Eventually, I put down the remote and surrendered completely. The veil was removed, and the chains of spiritual bondage were broken. I know I could easily be hooked again, but I also know God is in the business of restoring souls, in helping us pass the test of true repentance. The Lord wants all of it: our minds, hearts, families, and relationships. He wants all because He is jealous enough to do anything to save us—even die on a cross.

Some may think, *Okay, Jacky, so you struggled with TV— what's the big deal? Aren't we supposed to veg out and enjoy life—not take it so seriously?* Yes. Of course, life is to be enjoyed, but we must remember that what is permissible is not always beneficial.[9] Neither is it good to do what God commands us not to do. But we tend to find a way to justify doing those things anyway. Wouldn't you agree? We don't like to deny ourselves, and we want things when we want them. However, because The Lord planted eternity in our hearts, we must keep in mind just how restless our hearts can become. They were made for more. We can't be complacent or go to extremes, but we should account for what will lead to other things. It's so easy to enjoy things and be okay with a small compromise here and there. But what's lacking? What allows this boredom with Christ to creep in? What's lacking may well be our conviction of sin and our need to return to the Lord.

United Back

Even though we struggle with tension and compromise, the Lord still wants us to come back to him: EVERY. SINGLE. TIME. Psalm 40:17 (AMP) says:

> *"Even though I am afflicted and needy, still the Lord takes thought and is mindful of me. You are my help and my rescuer. O my God, do not delay."*

He sees our heart and knows something valuable is buried beneath all our compromise and lack of commitment. That is so comforting, but how is it possible? The Bible gives a perfect example with the prodigal son. In the story, we see dark thoughts creep into the son's heart, and he questions whether he can truly trust his father. The son has to choose—cashing out, he leaves his father—spending all he has on worthless things. After a long journey and realizing how far he has fallen, the son arises from the filth to begin the long journey home. Weak, barefoot, broken, almost dead, he is revived in coming home. With open arms and love, the father is excited that his son has returned. As we see in this story, the father never stopped loving his son.[10]

Life can't be about acquiring things or finding ways to be entertained. The conflict we feel is there because of the value or importance we give to things that really don't matter. This culture will always demand our attention and focus. The question is, will we use the Lord's strength to battle the war? Do we need the Lord to change our heart? Because He will if we ask. Deuteronomy (AMP) 30:6 says:

> *"And the Lord your God will circumcise your heart and the hearts of your descendants [that is, He will remove the desire to sin from your heart], so that you will love the Lord your God with all your heart and all your soul, so that you may live [as a recipient of His blessing]."*

We have the chance to gain a whole heart—one that is not easily divided. True devotion unwilling to compromise is possible. Our souls have a longing to be filled. That's how God created us! Instead of one-foot-in, one-foot-out, let's jump all-in with unwavering devotion and keep our eyes locked on the Father. When we do, we see his radiant love for us and His work through the unexpected. Our brokenness, although unexpected and painful, is the Lord changing us into something better.

CHAPTER 3

Can't Rise Up: Broken Hearts

Flossing is a scam.

Growing up, I never developed the habit to floss and never saw the benefit in doing so. I mean, every dentist visit seemed the same, and a perfect gum line was never obtainable—so, *why floss?* I know this is probably gross, but eventually the habit clicked. After a perfect record without cavities was crushed and I received my first crown, I realized I needed to floss. Or I was going to have changes that were not good for my health. Avoiding the habit for most of my life, I finally had to cave. The pain was excruciating, but I kept trying. At one point, I felt my heartbeat inside my mouth—the throbbing pain was so bad. Finally after three weeks with bleeding, agonizing pain, and wanting to give up, I made progress. My pain subsided, and flossing became a habit. My diligence because of the pain paid off! This made me consider how true this is with life and suffering. Sometimes, we need to fail to find restoration. There are times when we will ache, bleed, and feel lost. It's in those hard and unbearable moments that we see there is someone greater who will pull us through. We find that when we fall, which we all do, healing is possible—so we can rise again.

Charles Spurgeon once said, "There are many sorts of broken hearts, and Christ is good at healing them all."[11] The fight to free yourself from brokenness is not easy. There are choices and sins that interfere with our healing. Maybe there's an illness, the loss of family, a job, a friend, parenting struggles, addiction, or weight struggles that intrude. The list could go on, but the point is, every heart on this earth has been broken. We are imperfect, weak people that will break and bleed for many reasons. Our weary spirit and dwindling confidence needs comfort, peace, hope, and most of all, someone to pick us up when we fall.

Good God Expected

No one is exempt from brokenness, which makes us wonder why suffering is inescapable. When our hearts are broken, we try to remove the shattered pieces as quickly as possible. But God wants those jagged pieces saved so He can reshape and mold us into what He wants us to become. This molding, sculpting, shaping, and refining is necessary, or we would have no need for a perfect Savior. Sometimes, I wonder if we knew what the exact hardship would be before it came, would it make the eventual brokenness any easier to understand or accept? No, it wouldn't. Jesus reminds us that in this world, we will experience tribulation, yet we should take heart because He has overcome the world.[12] We have to continually remind ourselves that Christ is good, does good, and works everything for our good and for His glory.[13]

A question heard often is, do we have a God that is good all the time? It's easy to say, "He is good" when a good outcome appears. But what if our expectations, the things we prayed so hard for, never happen?

- The loved one who never healed

- The job or opportunity that never happened

- The loss of everything we have: friends, family, money, reputation, etc.

- The needs or wants that go unanswered

We can relate to all of these in some degree, right? Our expectations for a good God never allowing bad things to enter our lives gets flattened; therefore, we question, mourn, and wonder why we tried to have the faith that moves mountains. After all, don't we just need a little mustard seed of faith?

Not long ago, I gave birth to our second son, Jack. The delivery of our first born, Jameson, had left me completely frightened of childbirth. The confidence I thought I gained dwindled as it drew nearer. Why did I think I could do this again? I don't know, but here I was preparing for the worst. After hemorrhaging with the birth of Jameson, which took them an hour to fix me up, the doctor informed me I would need a blood transfusion, or a heart attack could happen at any moment. My heart already racing, the doctors moved fast, poking and prodding, reviving my half beaten body back to health.

Remembering my first experience led me to begin fervently praying for a different outcome this time. I needed reassurance that those scary events wouldn't happen again. In the weeks leading up to Jack's birth, with increased anxiety, I pleaded, *"Jesus, are you with me?"* I remember saying, "Okay, God, the first delivery was pretty rough, so I'm gonna pray hard that this one is smoother. If you could please listen to my prayers and answer them, I will give you all the glory, sharing what you have done."

I had faith. I trusted Him. I knew He was good, and I
knew He would pull me through. But I guess you could say
I made a special agreement with God. Anyone else ever ask
for one of these? With my agreement set, baby number two
was on its way. I was scared, but I knew this time would be
different. I often repeated to myself, "*God is good. God is good.
He's got this.*" Eventually, the time came, yet not every prayer
was answered. In fact, I had to endure similar hardships. My
body was brutalized again. After two days of intense labor,
pushing for three hours, we realized Jack was stuck. A cesarean
section was the only option left. Crying from pure exhaustion, I could still hear God saying, "*I'm here, Jacky. I will not
leave you.*" I made it through surgery, and a new little boy
waited for his mom to hold him. My battle wasn't done—I
had another blood transfusion. This time, it took eight tries
to find a vein—it was excruciating. I sat there, numb—trying
to keep the stream of tears under control. Finally, a line was
established, and my recovery began. Still, I wondered why this
happened again. Both experiences shook me, and both left
me with a question and a choice: *Is God still good?*

I want to take a moment here to say how grateful I am to
have two healthy babies, and I don't take them for granted
one bit. I did, however, mourn my expectation and thoughts
of how God was going to pull me through this experience.
I questioned. I wondered. I tried to figure it out. But in the
end, I realized God *did* have my back. His mercy blew me
away. It just took me a minute to realize. Yes, this second
labor was just as scary and tough as the first, but I saw how
He provided strength and comfort. I regained my clarity after
all the grogginess to see how sovereign He is. I had to rack or
reset my focus—a term my husband taught me about cameras.
When you rack your focus, you purposely go out of focus,
then go back in for a sharper one. I had to change my focus
to come back again and see the sharper picture—to see the
good of the whole. Max Lucado said, "We must allow God

to define what is good. That too often our definition includes health, comfort, and recognition. God's definition, in the case of His son Jesus Christ, the good life consisted of struggles, storms, and death."[14] From Christ, we see that good was there all along—Not in how we see it but in how it was seen on the cross. The greater good was to sacrifice for our salvation and for His glory. In the midst of our brokenness, we can always return to the character of God and know His arm is holding us up. Always remembering, He will never leave nor forsake us.[15] Sometimes, we have to go through tribulation, maybe something horrible and tough, so when we arrive on the other side, we can remember the gift of Jesus and then help someone else do the same.

Be Unyielding

Turbulence: The rough, sometimes violent, unsteady movement that jerks our once calm state, leaving turmoil until it passes. If you're familiar with flying, you know at any point, turbulence can occur. I'm not a huge fan of flying, so when this happens, I grip the arm rest and close my eyes(praying fervently) while keeping the little blue bag on my lap—just in case. I've had flying experiences that get a little dicey, yet thankfully, the calm resumed quickly. Turbulence appears out of nowhere, just like some afflictions. We have no control over them in our everyday lives. Going through something, especially those things we didn't see coming, doesn't require us to turn off the engines when turbulence hits. It means we keep going through the rough spots until we arrive at our destination. In the pit of affliction, the lowest of lows, let's try to keep moving forward, instead of shutting down. When we look up—even when our hearts are breaking—we can lay claim to our nearness with God. He is everywhere. He knows what's going on in our lives. Even when our inability to feel God appears—let us still trust Him. Let's cling to that unyielding determination and stay with Him, even when we want to walk away or throw our hands up.

Job is a man who reminds me of reverent suffering. Who doesn't think of Job in the Bible, and the words "beauty for ashes" resounds in the mind? Sometimes, I sit and think about what this man went through. I can't wrap my brain around it. What brokenness, yet also, what faith, to endure the unbearable. Job lost everything—including his children—yet he never turned from God. Sure, he had moments of weakness, but overall, to see such brokenness be turned to represent God's glory is a beautiful account to read. Job kept examining his heart until he finally found the answer. Job 13:15 (ESV) says, *"Though he slay me, I will hope in him."* Although it may seem God did something contrary to His Word, what Job says is, he will still trust; he will still stick with what the Word says and what he knows to be true.

Job had an unyielding determination not to give up—not to throw the Christian life away—to fight when all seemed lost. We have to see in this story that God is the answer, and Satan is the problem. It has always been that way. Even when we are confused and think God is the problem—we must remember there are two different sides. God is faithful and just—always providing the answer to our problems. Therefore, we must fight this urge to pull away and give up. In the end, we see restoration for Job and how the Lord poured even more blessing on him. What a victory, after such brokenness, to say, "Even though you slayed me, even though I thought this was the end, I still trust and praise you."

We can also see Joseph as an example of unyielding devotion to the Lord. In *Genesis 39*, we see a man betrayed by his brothers, sold into slavery. He was a man far from home, unfamiliar with his surroundings, and facing the unknown. After arriving, Potiphar found favor with Joseph because the Lord was with him and had caused Joseph to succeed. We see on his crazy journey, Joseph was finally able to rise, and life would become easier for him. Everything indicated smooth sailing until temptation came his way. Potiphar's wife had eyes for Joseph and was determined to get what she wanted. "Lie with me," she said.[16] Joseph could have said yes, could have justified this decision, and could have reasoned that no one would know, except them. However, Joseph didn't cave. He went on high alert, refused the wife, and fled in the opposite direction.

Joseph's devotion to the Lord remained firm. He believed that to lie with her would not only be sinning against Potiphar, his master but, more importantly, against the master of his heart and soul. As a result, Joseph suffered false accusations from Potiphar's wife and imprisoned even while an innocent man. What we learn from Joseph is, he was a man of unyielding devotion. Through his devotion, even when broken or stressed or unsure of the outcome, Joseph still wanted to please the Lord. His primary concern was God in the midst of his own peril. Let's remember, when temptations come, they are from a fiercely hungry enemy. Hungry for our attention, our souls and our future—constantly seeking to devour our devotion to the Lord. We must resist. We must stay on high alert—rooted and established in the Lord.[17] We remember and rejoice in the promise that the Lord is victorious over all evil. The God of peace will crush Satan under your feet![18]

Boldly Weeping

Because we live in a depraved world, brokenness can come from the unexpected, knocking us off our feet. These experiences happen, but there's another part to brokenness we need to remember—the reality of sin. When was the last time we wept over our sin? Really wept? Repentance involves both the turning away from sin and the turning back toward the Lord. How is our heart's posture when returning to Him?

David reminds us how one can be broken and not beaten while demonstrating the way God delights in repentance. *Psalm 51:17 (AMP) says, "My [only] sacrifice [acceptable] to God is a broken spirit; A broken and contrite heart [broken with sorrow for sin, thoroughly penitent], such, O God, You will not despise."* In his downfall with Bathsheba and her husband, Uriah, David allowed sin to get the upper hand. Once called out, however, David responds with a broken and contrite heart. He turned to God first, prayed for cleansing, confessed the seriousness of his sin, then pleaded for renewal. Being a Christian doesn't mean we don't get discouraged or experience brokenness. Being a Christian means we have a relationship, plus fellowship with Christ, that shapes how we think and act about our sin in the brokenness.

Are we broken over the ugliness of our sin? Over the high treason we committed toward the Lord? We must remember: All sin is treason against God, not only sins commonly acknowledged but also those that seem acceptable before they are swept under the rug—like no big deal. Our thoughts, the way we speak, the way we see others, and the way we see ourselves can become acceptable sins, easily forgotten, and not handed over daily. We need to hand our sins to the Lord, not in shame and condemnation, but in Goldy grieving, boldly and broken. We come in full agreement over our sin and kneel in humble reverence—ready for correction and restoration.

Hebrews 12:5-7 (AMP) says:

> *"My son, do not make light of the discipline of the Lord, And do not lose heart and give up when you are corrected by Him; For the Lord disciplines and corrects those whom He loves, And He punishes every son whom He receives and welcomes [to His heart]." You must submit to [correction for the purpose of] discipline; God is dealing with you as*

with sons; for what son is there whom his father does not discipline?

Let's not be in the habit of going through the motions or forget what true repentance means. When we tune our hearts to see our sin, we can then tune them to see His grace. The cross becomes more lovely, more magnificent. The gift becomes more precious when we see the sacrifice once more. May we never forget the good news that brings joy for us all.

Now We Rise

The Bible is not only filled with endless testimonies, of bold, unyielding sufferers, but of the greatest sufferer and example, Jesus Christ. 1 Peter 2: 21, 24–25 (ESV) says:

> *"Christ also suffered for you, leaving you an example, so that you might follow in his steps...He himself bore our sins in his body on the tree, that we might die to sin and live to righteousness. By his wounds you have been healed. For you were straying like sheep, but have now returned to the Shepherd and Overseer of your souls."*

Through brokenness and suffering, the Word affirms the truth to God's people.

- It's through unexpected affliction that we gain hope from the God of all comfort, and through Him, we escape relying on ourselves to securely trust in Him, like it says in 2 Corinthians 1:3–1 (ESV).

- Although we may break from our sin, God says come with a broken and contrite heart and, according to 1 John 1:9 (ESV), *"He is faithful and just to forgive us our sins and to cleanse us from all unrighteousness."*

- It's through any pain that the Lord gives us the strength we need to not grow weary. Our suffering is not meaningless. With joy, we can know that suffering produces endurance which then produces character and hope, as it is stated in Romans 5:3-4 (ESV).

God's goodness will always rise to the top, and in these trying times, God's glory will be revealed. Psalm 66: 10–12 (ESV) says, *"For you, O God, have tested us; you have tried us as silver is tried. You brought us into the net; you laid a crushing burden on our backs; you let men ride over our heads; we went through fire and through water; yet you have brought us out to a place of abundance."* There will be times when we are angry, when we want to disengage, hide or run away, but we must lean into Jesus. We need to pray for our hearts to move beyond ourselves and to rest in the God of all comfort. From there, our brokenness can heal and we can lean into people. We welcome their prayers and allow them to walk beside us. By leaning into Jesus then others, healing can begin. We begin to see our afflictions are never wasted, and our pains are never meaningless. The Bible says in 2 Corinthians 4:16–18 (AMP):

Therefore we do not become discouraged [spiritless, disappointed, or afraid]. Though our outer self is [progressively] wasting away, yet our inner self is being [progressively] renewed day by day. For our momentary, light distress [this passing trouble] is producing for us an eternal weight of glory [a fullness] beyond all measure [surpassing all comparisons, a transcendent splendor and an endless blessedness]! So we look not at the things which are seen, but at the things which are unseen; for the things which are visible are temporal [just brief and fleeting], but the things which are invisible are everlasting and imperishable.

Every moment is preparing, working, and producing change. It is because of that growth that we do not lose heart. When we set our minds on the unseen weight of glory, we find a gift beyond all measure. When we fall, Jesus is the one who can help us rise again, even when we fall seven times.[19]

CHAPTER 4

Must Fix It: Fearful Hearts

There is always a choice.

My husband bought a new censor for the nursery camera when my almost three-year-old didn't want the purple light from the censor shining. My husband decided to add a piece of tape over it to hide the light. It worked. But, in doing that, the light made the tape hot and caused a fire. The fire alarm upstairs, while working, didn't react fast enough. We were in bed with my newborn beside me when I ran for my other son. The flames engulfed his room, and I was frozen, screaming ... then I woke up ... from my *daydream*!

My fears had taken form, as if they arrived from nowhere. In reality, the fear was inside me all along. It wasn't until I became a mom that my hidden fears revealed themselves. They ran deep, manifesting themselves inside my heart and mind. Over the last few years, God has used motherhood to show me why I react in certain ways, how I respond, and why

I need to change it. I know not everyone is a mother, but for me, motherhood is the one thing that brings my fears to life, enhancing them. Many fears center around my health, my kids, or my family. There are days when nothing is wrong—kids are great; husband is great; health, for the most part, is great; yet inside, the tension is so thick I honestly feel like I'm going crazy. It's something I can't explain, and when I try, I sound ridiculous. Deep down, I knew there was a problem, and I needed to get to the root quickly if I expected any chance for peace.

Sources Of Fear

Why do we fear? I ask this question a lot, and often, it's my lack of trust or need for control. Fear is a scary, living thing. There are many forms it can take. How we react to fear and our motivations matter. We have a choice to make. Which road do we want to travel? Fear or faith? First, we should consider the cause of our fears.

The unknowns and the what ifs: Often, fear sets in when we don't *want* anything bad to happen. We *know* suffering is real, but the thought of suffering happening to any of us seems unfathomable. Ever have a moment when you think about a friend or loved one dying? Your mind gets so wrapped inside the hypothetical scenario, and it begins to feel real. I admit, I've had several of these moments and would cry hysterically because I believed I had witnessed the unthinkable. But it wasn't real! Fear took over my mind, and once again, my peace was shaken. I was left with this wishy-washy faith that couldn't get a grip on truth.

The plethora of "what ifs" swirling around can become an endless maze of fears, causing us to try to take full control of the unknowns. When we don't trust God, we buy into the delusion and convince ourselves we can beat whatever comes our way alone.

In the Bible, I think of Abraham and Sarah. Remember when Abraham feared for his life and pretended Sarah was his sister? Not once but twice. Or when Sarah couldn't get pregnant, fearing she would always be barren, and God wouldn't come through? What does she do? She gives her maidservant, Hagar, to Abraham, then Hagar becomes pregnant.[20] Taking matters into our own hands never releases our fears.

The number and size of the battles: We may say, "The battle is too big", or "God won't come through." We believe He doesn't hear, see, or love us and wonder why the battles keep coming—one after the other. It feels like waves crashing over our heads, and afraid, we try to keep our head up, hoping we won't drown. It isn't until we remember the waves come in sets, and between them, there is a break. If we shift our mindsets, we see the victory between the battles, no matter how numerous they can be! Romans 8:37 (ESV) says, *"In all these things we are more than conquerors through him who loved us."* We can't allow fear to reduce the size of our God or to elevate the size and number of the battle(s) we overcome. The Lord gave us weapons: The Word and the Holy Spirit to fight against whatever wants to knock us down.

I'm reminded of Caleb and Joshua in the Bible. Here, these two men went with ten other spies to bring back a report on the land God had promised. Out of twelve, Caleb and Joshua were the only two who didn't report back with fear, instead offering hope and courage. The Israelites, however, accepted the fear from the majority and couldn't see the promise had already been given. All they had to do was believe in the promise. Sure, it was a little alarming to see and hear about giants. There was definitely a reason to be afraid, but they had the Lord with them every step along the way. The majority, choosing to fear, overtook the minority, choosing faith, hope, and courage. Therefore, they all missed out, wandering for forty more years.[21]

Changes in life: Sometimes, we cringe at change. The fear keeps us from stepping out to try something new and can cripple us into thinking failure is around every corner. Maybe the fear of change is like a cement block tied around our feet. We can't move forward because we drag our past with us into the future. There is so much baggage we carry with us, so much regret, yet it's never too late to change, to let go of that weight and be free. We have an unchanging God—which we'll dive into more in Chapter 5—for now, we need to recognize change can be exactly what God has in mind for us. We can make our lives more rewarding by being transformed into the image of Christ. We can't remain stuck or flatfooted.

I played volleyball in highschool, and the number one rule was to stay on our toes to be ready for the ball. Most sports are like this, requiring a ready or non-flatfooted approach. Being on our toes allows us to move forward faster. It allows us to react to the play and respond to the attack faster, decreasing missed opportunities significantly. Let's not allow fear to keep us flatfooted but on our toes, ready to move forward. Change is a *good* thing.

Don't Receive It

Last year, while driving on a long road trip, I noticed a billboard. I always notice those, probably because I think most are bizarre. One such billboard caught my eye—a certain theme park was advertised for an upcoming Halloween attraction. The tagline was "fear is waiting for you!" Uh, no thanks. I have enough fear without help from you. I guess I'm a little dramatic, but this made me think this is true in our everyday life. Fear is waiting for us like a lion looking for its next meal, devouring whatever it can. It wants to stalk, kill, eat, and destroy its prey. It wants us to stay numb, bear no fruit, hang on by a thread, or hope we can make it through the challenges alone. Fear has a way of sneaking in, making us feel vulnerable, and we don't even realize it until fear gives way to anxiety or some other emotion. Fear is the enemy. We can't stop fear or temptations from entering our lives, but we don't have to receive them!

Romans 1:17 (ESV) says, *"For in it the righteousness of God is revealed from faith for faith, as it is written, "The righteous shall live by faith."* God created us to experience fear to some degree because He created us to live by faith. Faith that is both the beginning and the progress of the Christian life; faith that presses forward, gaining victory over unbelief.[22] We can't allow fear to be the object of our faith. But, when we do, we need to reach for the hand that pulls us up.

My dad once shared how Peter walking on water was an awesome picture of how Jesus is the author and finisher of our faith. We see the disciples are in a boat, and a storm is raging. They anxiously try to figure out how to get out of the situation and end up panicking. They become disillusioned and discouraged—both a byproduct of fear. Then, they see Jesus walking on water toward them. Here is the part that gets me every time and is such a great example of faith in action in the midst of fear. Matthew 14: 28–33 (AMP) says:

> *Peter replied to Him, "Lord, if it is [really] You, command me to come to You on the water." He said, "Come!" So Peter got out of the boat, and walked on the water and came toward Jesus. But when he saw [the effects of] the wind, he was frightened, and he began to sink, and he cried out, "Lord, save me!" Immediately Jesus extended His hand and caught him, saying to him, "O you of little faith, why did you doubt?" And when they got into the boat, the wind ceased. Then those in the boat worshiped Him [with awe-inspired reverence], saying, "Truly You are the Son of God!"*

The *author of our faith* is the One who gave Peter the courage to step out of the boat. Once out of the boat, he steps forward, frightened and discouraged. Peter began to lose hope and trust by the second until the *finisher of our faith* reached out to pull Peter out of the abyss—restoring his soul. Jesus allows us to take the steps, allows us to make choices in life. We can choose to trust, even when it's scary and we see the enemy in front of us. We don't have to sink or drown, yet when we start to, Jesus is always there with an open hand—remaining the author *and* finisher of our faith.

Remember The Command

All through the Bible, we see those who were not fearless but had more faith to push past their fear. Noah, Esther, Joshua, Mary, Peter, women with the issue of blood, and Elijah. All these people had reasons for their fear, and while they did, they still believed and trusted God was greater than their fear. I have to be honest here: the command to "fear not" never hit me until now, and I've been a believer for a while. As I'm sitting here writing this particular chapter, the world is in chaos. This year, 2020, has faced many obstacles with everyone stuck, waiting to see what will happen. I'm sure many are reflecting during this time, but for me, fear is the number one thing I had to lay down. Like I said before, motherhood brought all these hidden issues forward, yet the events of 2020 created a pathway to healing for me.

At the beginning of this troubling time, I was ready to tailspin into fear, once again. Being overly anxious about anything health-related, this crisis played into my worst fears. At seven and nine years old, I had major hip surgeries. The memories of those still haunt me. That's likely the main reason I fear health concerns. But it goes deeper. I realized something, and I'm a little embarrassed to say, but I realized I feared death. Now I know there's a natural fear when we die, and I know

I will go to heaven. My fear was that I would miss out or go too soon, making me forget "fear not." I have always leaned on Isaiah 41:10 (ESV), but now I see it differently. *"Fear not, for I am with you; Be not dismayed, for I am your God. I will strengthen you, Yes, I will help you, I will uphold you with My righteous right hand."* The word dismayed jumped right out for me. It means to lose heart, spirit, basically sink in fear, and lose courage.[23] The bottom line: fear made me lose sight of eternity. Even if we died right now and even if we miss out on something important, we can "fear not" because

- God is with us

- He is our God

- He will strengthen us

- He will help us

- He will uphold us

According to 2 Timothy 4:18 (ESV), When we fully trust Him, He will deliver us from every battle — even if the battle brings us safely to the heavenly Kingdom.

The symptoms of life will keep coming, but we must not fear them. We put our faith in Jesus, because according to John 11:26 (AMP), *"Everyone who lives and believes in Him [as Savior] will never die."* For *"He will swallow up death forever; and the Lord God will wipe away tears from all faces, and the reproach of his people he will take away from all the earth, for the Lord has spoken,"* like Isaiah 25:8 (ESV) says.

The Greatest Cure

When Jesus died on the cross, it looked like all hope was lost. Maybe, what everyone thought and said was right all along. Fear lingered, and people who believed the truth about Jesus struggled to keep the faith. Jesus was the disciples' everything. Now, they feared for their lives after the crucifixion.[24] They became disillusioned and hid in fear, forgetting what the Lord said. Everyone was desperate for answers, and that's exactly what fear can do. It causes us to question, peering out from behind closed doors and hiding.

The resurrection changes everything. "Fear not" and "peace be with you" were the first words Jesus said.[25] Jesus had a plan bigger than just getting rid of the Roman Empire. Because of the cross, we are able to look past the fears and endure this world because the joy of heaven is set before us. Let's be like Jesus, who looked past the cross to the joy set before Him.[26] The fear of the Lord should be the only kind of fear we allow into our lives. We gain stability when we recognize and apply His wisdom and knowledge to help fight the darts Satan has thrown our way. We don't fear what the world is ready to hit us with, but we fear falling short of the mark God has set for us.[27]

Yes, the Lord will fight for us. The battles are His. But we are still in the fight and can't be caught flatfooted. Like God instructed Moses at the Red Sea, to tell the Israelites to move forward, He is also telling us to get moving![28] They didn't need to be idle spectators but to run like crazy to escape the Egyptians. No matter how frightful the future looks, how desperate we become for answers, God has already been there. We cast our fears on the Lord, and He will sustain us![29]

CHAPTER 5

All Alone and Forgotten: Discouraged Hearts

The three letter word: WHY?
    Ever wonder *why* God allowed things to happen or not? Our *why* questions get no response? We wonder what we did wrong or how this plays into the future. Maybe feelings of being alone or forgotten start to disillusion how we feel about God. Take heart—no one is alone.

Discouragement leads to questions, confusion, and doubt. It's such a lonely battle. If we aren't careful, it could also lead to isolation and defeat.

- When people disappoint us

- When we are criticized or slandered

- When we fail

- When our expectations aren't met

- When prayers aren't answered

- When we take on a bodily illness, leaving us feeling hopeless and trapped

- When life isn't what we thought it should be

- When we feel disappointment with God and start to wonder if we *can* really trust all His promises

Discouragement stems from many things. If we don't know our unchanging God and His unchanging Word—if we aren't firmly built on the rock—then we won't be able to withstand the floods and torrents that come our way.[30]

Unchanging God

Two years ago for the Elwood family reunion, we tried to pick a fun place to reunite. Lake Tahoe became the chosen destination—known for its crystal blue waters and comparison to paradise. We hunkered down on a sandy edge of the lake, excited to take in the relaxing beauty. The water was perfect, and we welcomed the opportunity to snorkel or swim without fear of a great white lurking. *Yes, another fear not mentioned in the previous chapter.* Let's just say, oceans are not my favorite place to swim these days. So, this place was a dream! As our family played along the edge of the lake, I had a chance to get in the water and snorkel a bit. Rocks were positioned everywhere. It was as if they were plopped into the perfect formation for swimmers to visibly acknowledge without problem. These rocks became vantage points as I took to swimming—points of reverence to remember where I was since they never moved. Even when the waves emerged from boats passing by, the push would move me, but I always found my way back with the unchanging rocks. As I rested on one particular rock, defogging my goggles—and to gain strength before I took off again—I remembered I could always come back, and the rock would still be there.

There is no rock like our God. Deuteronomy 32:4 (ESV) says, *"The Rock, his work is perfect, for all his ways are justice. A God of faithfulness and without iniquity, just and upright is he."* God is the rock, and we are the rushing waters that keep changing. The things we think won't change will, and that's *why* we become discouraged and lose our confidence. We feel forgotten and alone. We want something in our lives that is steady, something that will not falter—a fixed reference point to go back to. That's why we must put our faith and trust in the only One who will never change.

We cannot place trust in ourselves, in people, or the things around us because no one has full view of the future. The things of this world are always subject to change. That is why our unchanging standard needs to be God's Word, the message that never changes. For, according to 1 Peter 1: 24–25 (AMP), *"All flesh is like grass, And all its glory like the flower of grass. The grass withers And the flower falls off, But the word of the Lord endures forever." And this is the word [the good news of salvation] which was preached to you."* If our foundation remains secure in the Lord, then suddenly, life will take on a whole new dimension.

God's essence, His whole character, His attributes, His counsel gives us comfort. The way He thinks about us, the way He thinks about sin, the way He shows mercy, and gives wisdom is everlasting.[31] The God who created the earth and everything in it, He is the God who doesn't become smarter one day, then dumber the next. He doesn't get better or worse. He knows the future before we encounter it, and our *why* questions never take Him by surprise. Malachi 3:6 (AMP) says, *"For I am the Lord, I do not change [but remain faithful to My covenant with you]."* The more we are anchored in His Word, the *why* questions begin to fade, and we can grab hold of the faith and confidence that brings us to where we recognize the true rock. This rock, Jesus Christ, is our firm foundation, shield, fortress, and hightower.[32]

Trade Confusion With Confidence

I don't know about you, but I used to wish I could live in Bible times. I thought life would be so much easier. To be able to see Jesus, physically walk alongside him and witness what the disciples and people of that time did—I would never feel discouraged again. This, however, is definitely not the case. Throughout the Bible, we see several examples of discouraged people. People who felt lost, forgotten, hopeless, and alone. We see people who took risks and were criticized and people who had failed and wrestled with God's plan. Discouragement is everywhere in the Bible, rubbing up against the miraculous stories of healing and deliverance. People of the Bible are just like people today: one day succeeding in faith and exuberance, the next day discouraged with confusion and doubt.

Habakkuk was one such man, faced with choosing confidence. A famine had hit the land, and an all-too-familiar question arose. *Why* did Habakkuk have to go through that? This same question is asked by many, even believers in Christ. Isn't this Christian life supposed to be easier? Why do we have to go through that? Aren't we supposed to get the answers we prayed for in the timeframe in which we prayed? Habakkuk 3:17–18 (AMP) says, *"Though the fig tree does not blossom and there is no fruit on the vines, though the yield of the olive fails and the fields produce no food, though the flock is cut off from the fold and there are no cattle in the stalls, Yet I will [choose to] rejoice in the Lord; I will [choose to] shout in exultation in the [victorious] God of my salvation!"*

We see here that even Habakkuk didn't have all the answers and didn't understand *why* this was happening. Even if he did know, do we think he would understand all God was doing? Our minds will never be able to comprehend all the Lord does.[33] The situations we are in now may very well feel like nothing seems to be working, especially when the furnace is hot, and the lions are ready to feast, until we remember who our God is! He is faithful and dependable, standing with us through it all. Let's do exactly what Habakkuk did. He chose to rejoice and follow God. Habakkuk 3:19 (AMP) says, *"The Lord God is my strength [my source of courage, my invincible army]; He has made my feet [steady and sure] like hinds' feet And makes me walk [forward with spiritual confidence] on my high places [of challenge and responsibility]."*

John the Baptist was another who struggled with discouragement. He goes from being Jesus' forerunner to being put in prison, eventually leading to his death. In the midst of imprisonment, we see him question *why* he is there and sends his disciples to ask Jesus a question. *"Are you the one who was to come, or should we expect someone else?"*[34] By asking this, we see that John wanted and needed clarification. He was becoming disillusioned. After all, the Messiah was supposed to judge sin, overcome wickedness, and bring about His new Kingdom, yet this part did not make sense to John. Instead of giving John a direct yes or no, Jesus answers back with truth John should already know.[35] Jesus said to them in Matthew 11:4–6 (ESV), *"Go and tell John what you hear and see: the blind receive their sight and the lame walk, lepers are cleansed and the deaf hear, and the dead are raised up, and the poor have good news preached to them. And blessed is the one who is not offended by me."*

Jesus wanted John to go back to the basics in the midst of discouragement. He wanted him to remember and see what was still happening, instead of leaving him high and dry. Jesus wanted him to confidently know Christ is the Messiah, and that would never change. I don't know if this brought comfort to John, as he still didn't get a direct answer to *why* he was in prison, but he had the ability to remember and had the answer from the past. Just like Habakkuk, John the

Baptist, in the midst of disillusionment and discouragement, needed to have confidence in where he had been, who Jesus was, who He is, and will still be to come. We see that, even if we are discouraged and confused, we can't allow our hearts to linger in those places. We can't miss out on who Jesus is, who we are in Him, and what is still happening around us. It can be hard, seeing what goes on around and in us, yet Jesus is living, active, and full of power.[36] Though we have not seen or physically walked alongside Jesus, like John the Baptist, we still fix our eyes on what is unseen. We can know Jesus and know He is always working out something indescribable. In the discouragement, we don't give up or lose heart but learn to wait on Him.

Don't Run; Wait

All the answers we long for may not come, but we don't give in, and in the waiting, we mustn't grow faint. Matthew 24:13 (ESV) says, *"The one who endures to the end will be saved."* Hannah knew what it was like to overcome bitterness and faithfully wait. After being barren, provoked, and ridiculed, you can understand how bitterness could easily enter a heart. The *why* answers to the longing questions she didn't see coming, but the Lord heard Hannah's cry. He saw her heart and opened her womb. It was in the waiting that brought about the maturity she needed to not grow faint. Hannah kept her heart open before the Lord, and remained established on the Word. She found her only security in life when everything around her wavered. 1 Samuel 2:2 (ESV) says, *"There is none holy like the Lord: for there is none besides you; there is no rock like our God."*

The easiest thing is to give up. If we give up, then the enemy has won. If we become bitter, like Hannah did at first, it's as if we have joined the enemy. To quote a viral youtube video, "Ain't nobody got time for that!"[37] Thankfully, Hannah turned it around and showed us her heart. While waiting, she prayed, and we see before she got an answer, before she got anything from God, she gave Him all the glory. She gave back before God gave her a precious son as a gift.[38]

All my life, I felt a little bit like Hannah. The feeling that you have been forgotten, that you've been passed over, and someone else always got your spot. I remember in high school not making the soccer team. The decision boiled down to me and one other girl, a girl who had never played before, but because she was more popular, she got picked. I was crushed, not because I was the best but because I worked hard to be part of a team. After several tryouts and the first cut not making the last hurdle, bitterness, confusion, and of course, discouragement left me feeling not enough again. Even though I eventually looked at the situation positively, I realized this situation had played out in various ways throughout my life—especially in the Christian circle. I can't explain it, but I have felt that things are harder for me. The typical questions would appear: *Why* someone else was this or that—or has that ministry or opportunity and I don't. You know, those kinds of questions. When I finally clued into my attitude and heart issue, I realized how much prayer and contentment I lacked. My heart needed to wake up. It needed to walk away with peace, knowing that because something is hard doesn't mean it's not worth it. My heart needed to acknowledge that anything I receive in life—an opportunity, a family, friends, etc.—is to be enjoyed while giving glory back to the Lord. The question remained: *would I really give back what He gives me?*

Here are some prayers we can go to when waiting:

1. Lord, help us not to lose heart. Help us to physically do nothing while waiting for the answer. Put the desire in us to pray and read the Word with urgency. Like Revelation

3:11 (NKJV) says, *"I am coming quickly! Hold fast what you have, that no one may take your crown."*

2. Lord, awaken our hearts. Like Abraham, allow us to firmly believe your promises and have no unbelief in doing so. According to Romans 4:20 (NKJV), *"He did not waver at the promise of God through unbelief, but was strengthened in faith, giving glory to God."*

3. Lord, help us to not take matters into our own hands but trust you have a plan. Isaiah 55:8 (ESV) says, *"For my thoughts are not your thoughts, neither are your ways my ways, declares the LORD."*

4. Lord, we pray for confidence. We pray that when times get confusing and we become discouraged, we can remember to go back to what we know. In Romans 15:13 (ESV), it says, *"May the God of hope fill you with all joy and peace in believing, so that by the power of the Holy Spirit you may abound in hope."*

5. Lord, we pray we can live by the fruit of the Spirit. It says in Galatians 5:22–23 (AMP), *"But the fruit of the Spirit [the result of His presence within us] is love [unselfish concern for others], joy, [inner] peace, patience [not the ability to wait, but how we act while waiting], kindness, goodness, faithfulness, gentleness, self-control. Against such things there is no law."* Help us see our training in progress. Amen.

Training Up A Champion

Lester Sumrall said it well: "Anyone who is willing, can be a champion for God."[39] Do we see ourselves as champions for God? Do we want to be a champion for God? What does that look like, and what type of training is necessary? Nehemiah is the perfect example of a man whose foundations were solid.

His character set him apart, and that was the main reason God used him, and he was tasked with rebuilding Jerusalem's walls. It was the time spent in secret, his intimacy with God, that trained Nehemiah to become a champion for the Lord, and the Lord was with him through the calling. For God, it wasn't about position or titles, it was about a regular person who had a heart for Him. Nehemiah refused to compromise, had moral integrity, and was faithful. We can learn a lot from the story of Nehemiah, but his beginning response, through prayer, sets the stage for the foundation we must all have to make Godly training worthwhile in the long run.

The first thing Nehemiah did upon hearing the discouraging report of the walls was sit down and weep. This part alone shows Nehemiah's heart. He knew this was more than just the fallen rubble needing to be rebuilt. It was about sin. He knew that to rebuild, he first had to weep over what was broken, followed with fasting and praying. We come to see Nehemiah's prayer as a whole and what a champion should look like. It's in this prayer that Nehemiah acknowledged God's greatness, confessed Israel's sins (including himself), and requested God's help.[40] Even through discouragement, Nehemiah's deep feelings and compassion is a great example of how we can approach trials that come our way. We can see that prayer is the very thing that guides us. It allows us to see clearly the decisions we should take and how to go about them. It's the privilege we have to come to the throne of grace, confess all our failures, while giving God the glory, and receiving His promises and guidance. The victory we have in our prayer lives is the ultimate victory that makes us champions for the Lord.

Whenever I see discouragement creep in, causing me to grow faint, I know my prayer life needs attention. A tool used to help me remember God's faithfulness is journaling. When I go long periods without significant prayer, inner tensions begin boiling to the surface, waiting to be released. That's why I take to paper, dumping whatever has been building up inside. All my emotions are laid out in a way only I know makes sense, allowing the Lord to make His way to my heart. Journaling allows me to remember. I look back at times and am shocked at all that God has answered. Not every prayer request was granted—and probably for good reason—but the majority were. Why was I shocked? Our God wants us to have that experience every day of knowing where our fixed dependability comes from.

Through prayer, we demonstrate that we understand the Lord's sovereignty and can trust in His leadership. It's where convictions and character are built to maturity and where God is glorified by responding specifically to our prayers.[41] Ever notice how much we are energized and strengthened when He grants our requests? Prayers support our faith and give us the confidence to keep taking righteous leaps for God. Even Jesus prayed earnestly, and the ultimate reason for prayer was to draw His power from the Father.[42] That should be our goal, too, since we can do nothing in and of ourselves.[43] When prayer is the number one thing we turn to, we can push through the rubble and allow God to restore and mold us in a way that can impact many. The cross needs to be our home base, our reference point, so we can function the way we were supposed to. Let us open our hearts to the ways of Christ. The One who restores our soul and leads us in the path of righteousness, all for His name's sake.[44] Like Nehemiah, let's learn to be people after God's own heart.

Part One
Reflections for the Heart
Chapters 1–5

Review: Looking back at the hidden dilemma and the problems that have been revealed, we can't function under a calloused, divided, discouraged, fearful, or broken heart any longer. We don't dismiss the fact that these momentary troubles will knock us down, but we can rise again! We rise by recognizing a full-functioning heart needs Jesus. We must always come boldly and regularly to the throne of grace because restoration is what can transform us from the inside out.

Coming up: As we move forward, we dig a little deeper. We regain focus on the kind of heart Jesus desires us to occupy. It will take change. It will take perseverance and a faith that has the *"assurance of things hoped for, the conviction of things not seen,"* according to Hebrews 11:1 (ESV). We can do this: We can have a heart for God and others by magnifying Jesus and never losing sight of the gospel.

Discussion Questions

- What type of damaged heart might you have? Are you able to recognize which parts need restoration and transformation?

- Do you recognize how powerful you can be in the Lord? Are there places where you still buckle—blinded by what the Lord is trying to teach you?

- Do you have divided loyalties? What is captivating your heart? Is it Jesus? Do you come back to Jesus when you realize your true devotion, or do you run, never to return?

- Do you believe God is good all the time? Even when you were almost taken out by life's battles, do you still have that unyielding determination to not give up? How often do you weep over your brokenness, over sin? Do you come boldly, asking for correction and restoration, or have you forgotten what repentance really means?

- Do you receive fear more than you receive peace? If so, what are you so afraid of? Do you know you have a choice not to accept fear?

- Do you know where your true confidence lies? Do you remember to go back to the Word in the midst of confusion? Do you welcome change in how you ask a question? Instead of "Why?" can you start the question with "How?" as a way to welcome prayer, endurance, and love for others?

  - How does God want to use the experiences in your life?

  - How can this help you trust God more and take a risk for Him?

  - How can this be used to help someone else? How can you give the gift of encouragement and hope that pushes out the clutter in hearts?

PART 2

Blessed Assurance

CHAPTER 6

The Ins and Outs Are God's: Transformed Hearts

"If Christ came back today, would you run and hide, or face Him with everything you have done and are doing in your life?"

It was during my first mission trip where my youth pastor asked this question. I thought I knew what it meant to follow Jesus, but in reality, I was confused, not fully understanding the depths of His love. All I knew was, I didn't want to be the one hiding. I wanted to belong to Christ and have confidence, knowing when I finally leave this earth, Jesus will be the One welcoming me home. My heart needed restoration, and a transformation that acknowledged everything from the inside out is the Lord's. I was given salvation, not from what I had done in life but because of what Jesus did on the cross. He paid it all, and while I was still a sinner, He died for me, and He loves me with an everlasting love. No longer do I need to rely on myself, but I now have His power, authority, and majesty to get me through the pressures of life until I finally go home to be with Him. From my sophomore year in high-school to now married with two kids, I find peace and hope in the fact that I've changed, but Christ has never changed. This transformed heart, although still a work in progress, can rest in the fact that Jesus is my blessed assurance.

The Simple Truth

As a Christian, a born-again believer, Christ changes every-thing. He is life in us, and this is when turning inward is a good thing. It's when we take moments to bask in remembrance of what He did for us and acknowledge His very words can transform a heart in an instant. My own testimony shows how all it can take is one question. One question broke through the walls of my heart. God knew the very moment when I would awaken, and clarity would serge through me. That question saved my life and brought me to Jesus. I have known other people and have read stories about similar things happening. Even the most intellectual, critical, hard-hearted person can be brought to their knees and given life from the One whom they have resisted for so long.

Someone who was once made of stone can be given a heart of flesh. This is how the Word changes people. All they need is the simple truth of the gospel. God alone changes hearts, and the Holy Spirit lifts the veil from our minds and hearts. Romans 10:9 (AMP) says, *"Because if you acknowledge and confess with your mouth that Jesus is Lord [recognizing His power, authority, and majesty as God], and believe in your heart that God raised Him from the dead, you will be saved."* What a God we have to give us all the chance to recognize and believe in our hearts that He is the way, truth, and life! I weep often at this thought, not because I'm trying to be over spiritualized but because I try my hardest to grasp daily what Christ has done for us all. He didn't have to save us. He didn't have to endure all that He did, but that's exactly what happened. The Lord made a way for sinners, sinners who can now be saved by grace.

I think about Paul in the Bible. He was a man who hated Christians, who killed them, yet God still went after him and captured his heart. How do you explain that? God loved him, pursued him, and used him. Paul didn't even see it coming! This man did a complete 180-degree turn and never looked back.[45] There is none too lost, too confused, too guilty, or too sinful who can't belong to Jesus. If you belong to Jesus already, there is none too lost, too confused, too guilty, or too sinful who can't come back. Everyone has a chance. It's not too late. God shows mercy daily, and His promises are there for the taking. All we have to do is receive.

We have seen that our hearts can become calloused, divided, broken, fearful, and discouraged, but there is a cure. This cure can turn hearts of stone into hearts of flesh, like mine and so many others. That cure is Jesus.

- He was mocked, beaten, and marred for us.[46]

- He was rejected for us.[47]

- He was nailed and hung on a cross for us.[48]

- He died and gave up His life for us. Matthew 27:50 (AMP) says, *"And Jesus cried out again with a loud [agonized] voice, and gave up His spirit [voluntarily, sovereignly dismissing and releasing His spirit from His body in submission to His Father's plan]."*

- He rose three days later for us! According to Matthew 28:5–6 (AMP), *"But the angel said to the women, 'Do not be afraid; for I know that you are looking for Jesus who has been crucified. He is not here, for He has risen, just as He said [He would].'"*

- He has rescued us![49]

Why?

He loves us that much. It's that simple. 1 John 4:9–11 (AMP) says:

> *By this the love of God was displayed in us, in that God has sent His [One and] only begotten Son [the One who is truly unique, the only One of His kind] into the world so that we might live through Him. In this is love, not that we loved God, but that He loved us and sent His Son to be the propitiation [that is, the atoning sacrifice, and the satisfying offering] for our sins [fulfilling God's requirement for justice against sin and placating His wrath]. Beloved, if God so loved us [in this incredible way], we also ought to love one another.*

From the moment the gospel was presented, the plan was set, and God reached out through His son, Jesus. Because the human heart, in its own pursuits, will end up empty, lonely, and deprived, Jesus offers us forgiveness and a relationship in a world that is lost and broken. He made a way when there was no way.[50] God made the move to bring us back to Himself, and that's the good news we have to share to the world. We can now see from a new lens that our sins have been paid in full, and righteousness was completed. The perfect obedience of Christ paved the way to know and love God fully. The treasure we have been longing for is right in front of us. The most magnificent thing about God's story is that we will forever be in His glory, completely fulfilled in Him. Whether we have been walking with Jesus a long time or have forgotten Him along the way, we engrain our hearts with this simple yet powerful truth daily (from Hebrews 4:12, AMP): "*For the word of God is living and active and full of power.*" Transformation is available because there was someone who sacrificed His life to save us all and now dwells in us.

The Power In Us

The Holy Spirit is the One who convicts, gives new life, dwells in, and gives power. The Spirit has a domino effect in changing lives. The more we live with confidence through the power of the Holy Spirit, the more we can experience the treasured gift Christ left. This is how we experience it:

We experience the power of conviction. In college, I was part of a highly renowned Christian organization and was learning how to share my faith more. I learned how not to be ashamed of the gospel, how to pray for hurting hearts, and how important it is to be confident in our walks with Jesus. Then, on one spring break mission trip, something clicked. (I realized we are not the ones that change someone's heart.) It was while talking to strangers on the beach that I realized it's not about me. It's not about us. (We can't make someone believe in Jesus, and why would we want to?) The Holy Spirit alone works in people's hearts. It's a supernatural act no man can do. We can share truth and plant the seed, but in the end, it's up to the Lord. Like my testimony earlier, the Spirit can move through a verse, a pastor, or even a stranger you happen to cross. The point is, the pressure is off, and our purpose is to be obedient. That was a revelation I have never forgotten.

We experience the gift of eternal life. By the Holy Spirit, the minute we accept Jesus into our hearts, the gift of eternal life is presented, and we are now the temple for the presence of God.[51] The Spirit dwells in us and guides us, wanting to be in our hearts permanently, while taking us deeper, maturing, and teaching us how to walk in holiness. For He is our *"Helper (Comforter, Advocate, Intercessor—Counselor, Strengthener, Standby), to be with you forever,"* according to John 14:16 (AMP).

We experience God's power in us. Romans 8:11 tells us the Spirit that now lives in us is the same that lived in Jesus as he walked this earth! Boy, do we need this power every day. We need it to combat the tensions, the attacks, and to overcome the world daily. Because the Spirit guides us in truth, we can then produce the fruit of the Spirit. That's our gauge for whether we are living by the Spirit. This will lead us with confidence to help lead others.

I always think of the disciples whenever I think of God's power and the Holy Spirit. Do we ever think about the day of Pentecost and wonder what kind of light bulb went off in their hearts and heads? The day the Holy Spirit descended upon the disciples of Jesus arrived, it marked the beginning of the church's mission to the world. All of the sudden, these people, who went from being calloused, discouraged, fearful, and broken, never looked back. They finally got it! It clicked so much—these men were willing to die for it, and they did. Jesus left a mark and not just any mark. He marked their hearts with the Holy Spirit and with the joy of eternity set before them.[52] Nothing was going to stand in their way. They remained in fellowship with Christ while steadying their hearts over and over again. I'm sure they remembered the ultimate cost of Jesus dying for their sins and knew the primary purpose on earth was so important. Matthew 28:19–20 (ESV) says, *"Go therefore and make disciples of all nations, baptizing them in the name of the Father and of the Son and of the Holy Spirit, teaching them to observe all that I have commanded you. And behold, I am with you always, to the end of the age."* Let's be careful once we have our relationship with Christ that we don't slip from His presence and forget the good news. Let's remain steady, ready to take on purpose. Like dominoes, the effect of Jesus is still going before us and is still changing hearts today.

Beating Carnality

Carnality is when we become controlled by fleshly desires.[53] It's living a life that has the Holy Spirit dwelling inside but decides following Jesus is a bit too costly. As Christians, we should be aware we all have the ability to become carnal. That's what sin does. It easily allures us, capturing our senses, leaving no place sacred for us to grow in maturity. This is the exact issue Paul addresses to the Corinthian church in 1 Corinthians 3:1–3 (NKJV): *"And I, brethren, could not speak to you as to spiritual people but as to carnal, as to babes in Christ. I fed you with milk and not with solid food; for until now you were not able to receive it, and even now you are still not able; for you are still carnal. For where there are envy, strife, and divisions among you, are you not carnal and behaving like mere men?"*

As believers, the Corinthians never grew up. They lost their senses, forgetting the danger of the flesh. Their lives were welcoming the fake promises that needed to be uprooted, put to death, and replaced with God's truth—fast. Because the world was leaking into their hearts, it began influencing them in ways that kept them from maturing in the Lord. That's when Paul came in and called the Corinthian church out. Their lives needed to reflect the lives of a true Christian. The real problem with the Corinthian church was, they forgot the gospel. Their transformation in Christ had stalled, and their sin suppressed their appetite for more of God.

What's feeding our affections, causing carnality to slip into our lives? What are the empty promises we tend to hear that cause us to give into the illusion Satan wants us to believe? There are times I have found myself in these places where the invitation to sin once again was staring back at me. Food is a common area Satan uses, in his strategy, to destroy my appetite for God. He knows exactly how to talk to me, taunting me with the idea that being in the moment, the "right now," is all that matters.

- I earned this

- I need an escape

- Nobody will see/know

- Just one bite

- I won't die/It won't hurt anything/I can stop anytime

These lies come often, invading my heart, wanting that instant gratification food can give, but leaving me scrambling to find the right perspective. Sure, I could give myself whatever I want, I could eat whatever I want, which I have many times, but what was this feeding into? What are the long-term effects? Food fed my desire to be served. Instead of feasting on Christ, I gave into the junk that tries to satisfy but can't. My love/hate relationship with food was my area of weakness. That's why I need to understand this pattern of attack so I can guard against it. I'm sure this is a battle I will face forever, but I never want food to suppress my appetite for holiness. Maybe it's not food, but envy, jealousy, slander, gossip, hypocrisy, vulgarity, sensuality. These are all things we need to flee from and do no more. The Bible says in Romans 13:14 (AMP), *"Clothe yourselves with the Lord Jesus Christ, and make no provision for [nor even think about gratifying] the flesh in regard to its improper desires."*

As Christians, we never stop being broken, needy, desperate sinners who need God to supply grace. When faced with our failures and sin, it should be His mercy that moves us to repentance.1 John 1:9 (AMP) says, *"If we [freely] admit that we have sinned and confess our sins, He is faithful and just [true to His own nature and promises], and will forgive our sins and cleanse us continually from all unrighteousness [our wrongdoing, everything not in conformity with His will and purpose]."* Before we get to heaven, we may sin, but our aim should be to sin less, to not fall prey to the flesh. When we do make a mistake, when we give in to the illusion of sin, let's remember the gospel. Run to the throne of grace, not in guilt or shame but with hearts willing to do whatever it takes to not fall back. We kneel with hearts willing to receive the mercy Christ so freely gives in our time of need. He is the One who is faithful, the One who loves to the very end, and the One who still gives solid food that makes us strong.

Godly Thinking

Since our bodies are now the temple of the Holy Spirit, we are urged to offer them up as living sacrifices, holy and pleasing to God. We are then told, as our act of worship, how to do this. Romans 12:2 (NKJV) says, *"And do not be conformed to this world, but be transformed by the renewing of your mind, that you may prove what is that good and acceptable and perfect will of God"*

We hear this, saying, *Today's battles are fought between our ears.* What we take in, we think. Our mindset is under attack daily. As a result, our actions depict what we think and what's ultimately in our hearts. Remember where the source of human thinking came from? Sin started in the thought of Satan, not in action, and pride took over.[54] We need to remember that Satan wants everyone to think like him, act like him, and to ignore the example of Christ. Today, we become too easily consumed and distracted by the noise of this world that our minds can't think straight. From daily news, to current events, to the entertainment industry—they all strive to gain our thoughts and our attention. This can coerce us to think about things that end up consuming us. I'm all too familiar with this cause and effect. Sometimes, when I'm on social media, one scroll is all it takes to attack my heart and mind. The immediate blast from many views and opinions reignites fear, creates judgement, and activates my critical thinking skills. We all do this. We all search for knowledge on a continual basis. The problem begins when we make the world bigger, try to make it perfect, and in the process, forget to share how Jesus changed our lives. I often wonder why we put all this effort scrolling, posting, judging, and trying to fix earthly problems that can't be fixed. The Bible says in Matthew 24:35 (ESV), *"Heaven and earth will pass away, but my words will not pass away."* The ending has already been proclaimed; therefore, a mind set on things above will bring perfect peace, not as the world gives, but peace that allows us to breathe.[55] Isaiah 55:8–9 (ESV) says, *"For my thoughts are not your thoughts, neither are your ways my ways, declares the Lord. For as the heavens are higher than the earth, so are my ways higher than your ways and my thoughts than your thoughts."* No amount of reasoning or critical thinking skills will ever make us feel more secure than knowing our assurance is in Jesus.

The Bible is the main source that not only corrects our own reasoning but helps us filter everything. Because we consume information daily, even the good kind can become a problem. We look to the next book, the next sermon, the next influencer to fill us up and give us the answers. When we don't hear anything that instantly changes our lives, we get mad, blaming the person God called. Then, we end up right where we started. We forget to renew our minds with the main source. Books, podcasts, and influencers should be chosen wisely with discernment. We must keep asking whether the Bible is first. Some might say, "Jacky, I've heard this before. Go back to the source." But then, I ask, *Why are so many not doing this?* The questions that circle are

- What if I don't have time?

- The Bible doesn't make sense, so why try?

- How can I do this when I have kids to watch and/or things to get done?

- Other resources are easier, more entertaining, and relatable.

There it is.

These other resources are *not* the *source*. They should encourage, offer insight, and point us back to Christ to make us want to read the Bible ourselves. Sure, these resources can be super helpful, especially with little ones running around. I've been there myself. The point is, we need to be sure what we let into our minds is Christ-centered and that God's truth is absorbed into our hearts. Of course, there may be different opinions, but we allow the things that build up or complement what we already know to be true. A transformed heart has to be based in knowing Christ and being a true follower of His Word. We can't flip between what the world says and what the Word says. We must fight the urge to look everywhere except the Bible.

In this life, we either listen to the world or the Word of God. That's a decision we must make. The mind of Christ is obtained and maintained by taking the words out of scripture and engraving them into our hearts. We must take action and create this diligence permanently into our lives. When we start thinking like Christ, something changes on the inside. We start to truly transform, which is the key to Jesus having a permanent home in our hearts. The progression of God's ways is always at work making us more holy. The Word gives revelations we have never seen, it sharpens our focus to the cross, and shifts our minds to think more on God's level. To trust in the Lord with all our hearts and lean not on our own understanding, we must acknowledge Him in all ways, and He will direct our paths.[56] Do we have the mindset of Christ? Do we follow His example and recognize He's more than just an example? As we share in Christlikeness we have to be willing to sacrifice. Sacrifice is shifting our minds and guarding the hearts Christ has restored. In this world we are so used to being conformed, but God wants us transformed.

CHAPTER 7

See What Christ Sees: Soft Hearts

Difference of opinion, assumptions, misunderstanding, hurtful words. Ever experience these or given them to someone else?

When it comes to having a gentle heart toward others, we first need to guard our own. Guarding our heart allows us to have confidence in *who* we are and *whose* we are. Our vertical relationship always influences our horizontal ones; therefore, we need Jesus to be the Lord of our lives in all ways. He needs to be the One we love the most. Second, having a soft heart allows us to really see people for who *they* are and how God uniquely created *them*. Knowing God's character and how He thinks and loves will enable us to truly love those around us. In a world easily divided, we must grasp the importance of community and how much we need each other. This lack of unity is only a step away if we aren't intentional.

Divisions Doorway

Do we really understand God's love for us? Do we really love Him ourselves? Does He capture our whole hearts, or is He only allowed small sections of the whole? The fact is, if we really love and want the best for others, it shows in how much we love the Lord. In 1 John 4:20 (AMP), it says, *"If anyone says, "I love God," and hates (works against) his [Christian] brother he is a liar; for the one who does not love his brother whom he has seen, cannot love God whom he has not seen."* Often, we don't press into the great love of Christ until we lack love from others. Why is that? The Bible shows us time and again how much Christ loves us, yet we search for someone other than God to give the love we want and need. We forget that love came from Him first and is the purest, truest love there is.

Ephesians 2:4–6 (AMP) says:

> *But God, being [so very] rich in mercy, because of His great and wonderful love with which He loved us, even when we were [spiritually] dead and separated from Him because of our sins, He made us [spiritually] alive together with Christ (for by His grace—His undeserved favor and mercy—you have been saved from God's judgment). And He raised us up together with Him [when we believed], and seated us with Him in the heavenly places, [because we are] in Christ Jesus.*

Christians are not exempt from wayward feelings or desires. God created us with emotions and feelings, yet when we turn against others, when our hearts are starved for love, we have a problem. We yearn for more; we compare, become jealous, wanting what we can't have and, when we can't secure it, become bitter. The "if only" statements rise up from within, leaving us more confused and angrier. Pride says these reactions are not a big deal: that's how we should feel—but Christ says that's what will cause us to fall.[57] There are many wounds inflicted by others. We may have caused some wounds ourselves. It shouldn't be surprising that others will fail us. We should be prepared, yet with my own experience, it's still easy to be blindsided or knocked down. Our pride and desires, as well as assumptions and judgments, should be called into question. They show our lack of love for God and our lack of love for others. They are stumbling blocks to true unity.

How do we love others well? How do we love them always? *This seems impossible, right?* A question to ask whenever our hearts tend to sway toward bashing others or believing the worst: If we could foresee all the things others would do or say to us, but couldn't do anything about, would we still love them? This is a tough question, and I think in my mind and heart, I would probably hold this knowledge against the individual, knowing the dreaded future. This was not the case for Jesus. He didn't assume the worst; He knew the worst. Jesus knew who would betray him, abandon him, lead Him to the cross, yet he still loved us enough to die for us and rescue us from our sins. He had compassion, knowing deep down what we could offer to others, calling out the good and the bad in our lives in such a loving and bold way. Jesus always points back to the truth.

The ultimate love, the One we must take into account daily, is the love that died for us all on a cross. That's the kind of love we treasure, step out with faith, and take hold of. That's the love that keeps us from loving with only our eyes. When we love a person with only our eyes, it can become a disease, distorting the truth and leading us down a path of division, which needs an anecdote quickly. Luckily, we have the anecdote that heals our wounds and helps us love the way we should.

Our Responsibility

A soft heart rooted and established in the Lord *knows* when it's becoming hard-hearted. We can only fake being nice for so long. The ugliness eventually flows from our hearts into actions and words. As Christ followers, we have a responsibility to live in a way that honors God and others. Since the greatest and second greatest commandments involve both things, they clearly show how important they are to God. Here are some ways we can love better.

First, we pray. Seems so simple, yet a lot of us don't, or we forget. When I'm thinking about myself or how another person or situation is making me feel, especially in a negative way, I find myself wanting to turn away. It's hard praying for a person who doesn't care about the things I do, but prayer needs to be the first thing that comes to mind. Most of the time when I start praying, these feelings subside. Not all the time, but it's crazy how quickly reality can reappear, and the things that seem so big fade away. I can see the reasons why people do what they do, and I can give them the benefit of doubt. Better yet, I see my own negative heart, the grudge that has started to sneak in. Most of the time, we get in our own way.

The next steps we should take in loving others is to *listen, then ask questions.* We find out what's going on without forming an opinion. We listen to their concerns, their dreams, their ventures, and we see where their hearts are. We can't expect the worst and shouldn't anticipate we know best. We must be careful when it comes to this. None of us can know why the Lord called someone to do something different than we would. I have found sometimes people need to go through certain seasons to learn what should and should not occur. I've experienced hard lessons myself, things that needed correction for me to mature and move forward. We have to remember: Everyone's walk with the Lord is different, and only He can reveal specific guidance and truth to a person's heart.

After we have truly listened and seen their heart, then we ask the questions. We get to the core of what they want or think they need. Ask why they want or think they need this.

Ask them the tough questions. We need people in our lives who don't help us accept sin but people who lovingly and boldly call sin out. Living day by day with people we care about, means we can ask them what they need from our friendship and how we can best serve them. We enter the conversation knowing expectations could be unrealistic, but authenticity begins the moment we open up and let in. We need to know what our friends are most receptive to because we all have different pathways to receiving love and encouragement. I started doing this not long ago, and let me tell you, it's a game changer. Most people won't know how to take the question and might need some time to figure out what they actually need. It's okay—this is where breakthroughs happen in loving others well. Taking the time to see people, hear them, and love them the way they need will ultimately allow them to thrive and hopefully do the same for others.

The final act of loving others is to *speak life into them.* This should be the best part of any relationship. The truth of God's Word is life, and only that can satisfy the longing soul. We should aim to build up—not tear down; encourage—not destroy; correct—not abandon. Speaking truth softens hearts to want to live for Christ even more when inviting them to come along and do the same. Kind hearts want community—not competition; they want joy—not comparison; and ultimately want God to receive all the glory—and not have an ounce fall on themselves.

We have all missed the mark at some point. Others have failed us, and we have failed them. There have been many occasions I've wanted to isolate myself, ignore others, and would ask God to bring new people into my life. There have been times my heart ached, wanting certain friends. I wanted those who showed passion for the things of God and for the lost. As true friends, I wanted those who would love me for me, who would ask sincere questions, who would support me but also call things out that may be questionable in my life. I wanted those who actually cared and weren't just going through the motions of friendship. I wanted friends who would speak life into my soul and push me to see Christ in a whole new way. I became desperate for the perfect community of friends. Then, I realized I needed to be more desperate for Jesus, and wanting the perfect community became another idol. I realized my fists were closed, I couldn't let go yet wanted change, but God wanted me to open my hands. Open hands bring trust; open hands bring restoration and love. I needed restoration from the expectations I placed on others that only God could fulfill.

How do we gain restoration? When the hurts run deep or the pain takes years, can we find peace with a situation? Can we learn to trust again, to love again? Are we willing to forgive as Jesus forgave us? Forgiveness allows healing and the truest love to soften our hearts. It begins with us. We acknowledge what we did wrong and ask God to search our hearts for any hidden faults. All of this leads our hearts into true repentance.[58] Then, we forgive the person who wronged us. Ephesians 4:31–32 (ESV) says, *"Let all bitterness and wrath and anger and clamor and slander be put away from you, along with all malice. Be kind to one another, tenderhearted, forgiving one another, as God in Christ forgave you."* God's forgiveness takes the debris from our past, present, and future and wipes us clean. Because of that great forgiveness, we experience new mercies every day. New mercies not only for ourselves but for those who've hurt us the most.

Unity Matters

Unity with Jesus seems a breeze compared to the unity we should have with other people. The perfect unity with Christ is all we need, all we really want, yet fighting against different personalities and opinions constantly surrounds us. The vision, the reason we are here, is to share Jesus effectively and make disciples. When we lose this main vision, our mission to the world, we lose unity. Division is man made and is not from God. The sooner we realize this and fight against Satan's schemes to divide us, the stronger the body of Christ will become. Unity is such an amazing endeavor yet hard to keep up. But to be called one body, we should be excited and enthusiastic to be part of God's plan.

When it comes to unity, there is a question we should ask ourselves. Have you ever considered yourself to be something or someone special? It seems in Christianity, we hear, "God has big plans for us," or "We can be world changers." He does and we could, but how often do you interpret that as "I'm only special if I do something big?" What happens isn't what you expected; therefore, this makes you feel you aren't worth God's time or aren't particularly special, after all. We have the tendency to think others are making a bigger impact, so why can't we? Perhaps it's the other way around. We have a platform and influence, but look at others and think, *What are they doing for the Kingdom?* We can't think like this. The gifts and talents the Lord has graciously given are no greater or less than the person beside us.

In 1 Corinthians 12:12–20 (ESV), it says:

> *For just as the body is one and has many members, and all the members of the body, though many, are one body, so it is with Christ. For in one Spirit we were all baptized into one body—Jews or Greeks, slaves or free—and all were made to drink of one Spirit. For the body does not consist of one member but of many. If the foot should say, "Because I am not a hand, I do not belong to the body," that would not make it any less a part of the body. And if the ear should say, "Because I am not an eye, I do not belong to the body," that would not make it any less a part of the body. If the whole body were an eye, where would be the sense of hearing? If the whole body were an ear, where would be the sense of*

smell? But as it is, God arranged the members in the body, each one of them, as he chose. If all were a single member, where would the body be? As it is, there are many parts, yet one body.

The body consists of many parts; therefore, all the parts should realize they are special. Too many of us focus on the parts we want to be, instead of what God created us to be. For example, we strive to be the mouth because we think we can sing better, while God wants us to be the hand because he knows we can write with purpose. We lose sight of the vision doing this. I, too, have found myself thinking similar things, saying, "God has something huge for me to do. I can feel it, and I can't wait for it to be revealed." There was nothing wrong with wanting God to use me, but I missed the point God was trying to teach me. Yes, I am special to God; yes, I have a special purpose; but maybe my gifts and talents were meant to influence my small circle. I had to really think about why the body of Christ consists of different parts. What was my attitude towards the parts I wanted to be and the parts that were different from me? Too often, we try to be the same. We look down on certain parts, or think we have nothing to offer. In 1 Corinthians 12:24–27 (AMP), the Bible says:

But God has combined the [whole] body, giving greater honor to that part which lacks it, so that there would be no division or discord in the body [that is, lack of adaptation of the parts to each other], but that the parts may have the same concern for one another. And if one member suffers, all the parts share the suffering; if one member is honored, all rejoice with it. Now you [collectively] are Christ's body, and individually [you are] members of it [each with his own special purpose and function].

The source of focus for the church should be harmony, not eliminating diversity. Diversity is what keeps us functioning, and it helps mature us into seeing what is different, learning, and being there for others. There are always going to be things the body disagrees on, but most things we disagree on in life are not a heaven or hell issue. The Bible doesn't say believe in Jesus *and* something else. We, as believers, need to keep sight of the main vision, the special reason we are all here. Once we have accepted Jesus as our Lord and Savior, we have the Great Commission to run after. We then help others gain maturity in the Lord through discipleship. We do these two things while living above sin and being a witness to the people around us. These fundamentals get us to the prize! Philippians 3:14–16 (ESV) says, *"I press on toward the goal for the prize of the upward call of God in Christ Jesus. Let those of us who are mature think this way, and if in anything you think otherwise, God will reveal that also to you. Only let us hold true to what we have attained."*

The body needs to be strong and healthy to help more people. We are all special to God, working out what He has formed us to be. Let's not forget there are plenty of believers sitting beside us that are locked in bondage and have hearts that can't move past their own brokenness. Pray for them, be there for them, and most of all, remind them of who they are in Christ. Let's get back to full functioning order.

Begin And Master

Now that we know we are all special in God's eyes, we should never come to a point in life where we feel we have arrived. Where we think we have all the answers, we've figured stuff out, and know better than so and so. We've all been there, and that's pride talking, trying to sneak into our hearts. This is what happened to Paul during one of his many journeys. In Acts 21, we see that Paul made a great mistake in going to

Jerusalem against the will of God. The warnings came from multiple people not to go, but Paul's mind was set, and as a result, he was imprisoned. He later realized he had allowed pride to sneak in, and because he went to Jerusalem, it set him back many years in his ministry. We can learn from Paul by putting aside pride and arrogance, remembering we can all be deceived at any point, even if we are doing something for the Kingdom. Paul needed to regain a tender heart toward the will of God and others.

To gain a tender heart, we first remember what Christ has done for us. We remember the love poured out and the sacrifice that saved us from our sins. We focus on growing as a believer. We remain teachable. Mark 4:25 (AMP) says, *"For whoever has [a teachable heart], to him more [understanding] will be given; and whoever does not have [a yearning for truth], even what he has will be taken away from him."* We don't condemn others when they make mistakes and fall into sin. The reality is, we could all fall for similar things too. Instead, we continue in God's Word, asking questions and gaining revelations. Revelations from God's Word is what shifts our heart attitude and helps us mature. In Matthew 5:5 (ESV), even Jesus said, *"Blessed are the meek, for they shall inherit the earth."* Meekness means a person has inward peace, is spiritually secure, and worthy of respect. It's a person who is gentle, kind-hearted, sweet-spirited, and self-controlled. Having a meek, teachable spirit allows us to develop our fellowship with God that will lead to developing fellowship with others. The Thessalonian believers exhibited this, and because their faith grew in the Lord, they were able to keep increasing in their love for one another.[59] Love is a growing process. We won't always get it right, but when we do and are rooted in faith, the fruit that comes will be evident.

Just like the love we first received from God, we pour it into others along with mercy. Mercy is grace in action. It shows compassion toward others and offers a gift that brings unity to the body. Our mercy for others comes from God's mercy to us. Lamentations 3:22 (ESV) says, *"The steadfast love of the Lord never ceases; his mercies never come to an end."* I remember looking back on my life and thanking the Lord for His mercies. Why He handled things the way He did, I don't know, but what I do know is, the amount of mercy has never ended. There's no ending; like His love, it's forever. This should motivate us to give mercy to others, even when they may not deserve it, even when they are our enemies. I'm often reminded of the story of the good Samaritan. In the story, a man who was also a Jew, was robbed, stripped, beaten half to death, and left on the side of the road. He needed compassion and somebody to raise him back up. Both a Priest and a Levite saw him but didn't really *see* and kept walking. Eventually, a Samaritan came along who had an eye and a heart of mercy. He showed compassion in spite of enmity.[60]

That's the desire of God. It's not just that we have a special purpose and mission in this life. It's that we help raise somebody up in this lifetime. We may not have all the answers, we may struggle with our own desires and emotions, yet we remember what love and mercy did. They made us alive in Christ even when we were dead. For it is by grace we have been saved.[61] This is mercy and compassion on display. I pray we can give this to others and increasingly grow in love for each other. In 1 Peter 1:22 (AMP), the Bible says, *"Since by your obedience to the truth you have purified yourselves for a sincere love of the believers, [see that you] love one another from the heart [always unselfishly seeking the best for one another]."*

CHAPTER 8

Radiant Faces: Worshipful Hearts

Worship in prison?
For a semester in college, I had the privilege of leading worship each week in an all-male correctional facility in downtown Philadelphia. I probably wouldn't have said privilege to begin with; I just thought it would be a cool experience. Little did I know how that experience would change my life and my heart.

I will never forget the first visit. A team of six, including myself, traveled by bus to the facility. We shuffled through multiple security checkpoints while making our way to a room where a class was taught on possible weapons the inmates could be hiding on them. (You know, that knife and this blade thingamajig made out of a toothbrush … no biggie. Trying to conceal my wide eyed expression, I immediately regretted my decision.) As we made our way to the gym, I'll never forget what I felt next. I remember standing in this big circle almost like an arena with dark hallways going down every side of us. It was intense, and I felt uneasy as men yelled from their cells. We couldn't see them, but *they knew* what time it was and wanted to make it known.

Relief came when we finally made it to the gym, but then, there was another shift in intensity. Here we were faced with over two hundred men about to enter into a time of worship. My heart pounded. I was nervous yet excited at the same time. I think the hardest part was not being able to look these men in the eye. To me, the eyes tell a lot about a person, but rules needed to be followed, and we couldn't look the men in the eyes for our safety. Although I did my best to oblige, I snuck in a glimpse or two, and what I experienced was beautiful. There standing before me were so many worshipful hearts, so many radiant faces in the midst of pain, sorrow, and imprisonment. You see, the men who were able and chose to come longed for this time. Some of the inmates even played in the band with us while segregated to their side of the gym. It was awesome! The men who chose to be there soaked it all in and surrendered all they had left. They knew what time it really was and made it known for the Lord. Hearts that are willing—to not just see a service but to see the Lord—are hearts that long to make these moments count. This got me thinking about what it should look like when *we* enter a time of worship and enter the house of the Lord. Do we understand the meaning of worship? Do we see ourselves as true worshippers? What does it look like to enter into worship with hearts completely surrendered? A heart that is steady, that is ready to pay attention and grow to the next level is one that will find true intimacy and strength in the Lord.

Worshiper Identified

What is a true worshipper? People hear the word worship and often only think of singing songs. But worship encompasses everything we do. It's a lifestyle dedicated to the Lord in prayer, thanksgiving, fasting, giving, confessing our sins, and in reading God's Word. Real worship is a true view of God, one of reverential fear and awestruck wonder, and comes from the touch of the Holy Spirit living inside us. It takes both the head and the heart, thought and emotion, for a true worshiper to emerge. John 4:23–24 (AMP) says, *"But a time is coming and is already here when the true worshipers will worship the Father in spirit [from the heart, the inner self] and in truth; for the Father seeks such people to be His worshipers. God is spirit [the Source of life, yet invisible to mankind], and those who worship Him must worship in spirit and truth."* Worship is not just about the external reaction but the unveiling of the heart. Ever notice what happens when God's greatness gets absorbed? When we say, "I'm here, Lord—please take me deeper so I can see more of who you are." That complete surrender offers the most freeing release. I've felt this, and I'm sure you have too. We gain peace; we soften; we find joy; we become bold; we gain the courage and zeal that wants to glorify God in all we do. Why is that? Simple. We were made to worship and yearn for that intimacy everyday.[62] The door has been opened so we can have intimacy with Him. Are we ready? Can we walk into those sweet times and honestly say we surrender all we have? We should want to recapture the heart of worship regularly. We don't regain balance with emotion or thought but steadiness with both. With this, we continue to develop so we can reach new depths. Here are some ways we can do just that.

A true worshipper develops in secret. It's the time when no one is watching, when all we have is Jesus and our Bibles and remember who we worship and why we should worship. This secret place is the key to gaining the knowledge and wisdom from the Lord. It's where God opens the door to revelation and where cleansing, healing, and renewing occur. As we come to the well, there's an invitation to draw water, water that can quench any thirsty soul. We learn how to come to the well, then how to reach new depths, like Psalm 42:7 (ESV) says, *"Deep calls to deep."* The secret place becomes the deeper place where intimacy with the Lord lies. For the Bible says in Psalm 91:1 (NKJV), *"He who dwells in the secret place of the Most High Shall abide under the shadow of the Almighty."* The Lord wants to show us many things. It's in the still moments where we take our prayers and reverence to the next level, always seeing the Lord high and lifted up, knowing God's rightful place in our lives. Isaiah 57:15 (ESV) says, *"For thus says the One who is high and lifted up, who inhabits eternity, whose name is Holy: "I dwell in the high and holy place, and also with him who is of a contrite and lowly spirit, to revive the spirit of the lowly, and to revive the heart of the contrite."* We recognize that without Him, we are nothing. We have the ability to passionately pursue His presence all the time.

A true worshipper develops in their walks with the Lord. How awesome it is that the Lord reveals what we need to know from the Father and that He calls us his friend.[63] The Lord wants us to be His friend. Don't you love it when someone wants to be your friend? I know I do. This means we can know Him and in a way that grows our fellowship daily, becoming more intimate the longer we are in that fellowship. It reminds me of Moses. Exodus 33:11 (ESV) says, *"The Lord would speak to Moses face to face, as a man speaks to his friend."* Moses was called a friend of God because he knew the Lord and understood the ways in which the Lord had provided. Enoch was also someone who chose to abide in the Spirit and drink deeply from the well. In Genesis 5:21–24 (AMP), the Bible says he walked with God in reverent fear and obedience until the Lord took him home. Friendship takes time, yet it leads to recognizing grace so we are able to focus on the goodness of God and not always ask for something. We get to know God because His desire is for us to know Him face to face.

A true worshiper develops the sweet fragrance of Christ that reaches to others.[64] One of the most important things, as a worshipper, is to fan the flame. We can't have our hearts ignite during worship and not release it to others. We need to turn our awe, our amazement, the revelations we receive into a witness. People need our testimonies, to hear about God, to be encouraged, and they need to witness true Christians walking boldly in their faith. Everyone needs a drink from the well. Deep down, we all want to see a miracle, to experience healing and renewing. Some don't know what to look for or don't quite understand. Throughout the gospels, we see this. People were amazed. Not just by the supernatural and the healings that took place, but they were amazed by the ministry of Jesus. They saw something bigger than themselves and wanted to be part of it. It's incredible how living amazed and spreading that wonder to others can help us grow stronger in the Lord and stronger in serving the people around us. We have to make sure we never lose our wonderment of God.

Be Amazed

I have to repeat this to myself every second, every minute of every day. This Christian life, my faith, the church—all of it—it's not about me. It's not about us; it's about Him. Everything is about God's plan, His purpose, and His glory. In Revelations 14:7 (AMP), the Bible says, *"Fear God [with awe and reverence], and give Him glory [and honor and praise in worship], because the hour of His judgment has come; [with all your heart] worship Him who created the heaven and the earth, the sea and the springs of water."* The battle for our awe and amazement toward the One true God is a battle no one can escape. Our reverential fear for the Lord is in danger when we allow our hearts to become horizontally focused and stale to His magnificence. The worldly fear, the discouragement, the brokenness, the hard hearts, the pride—all of it can easily create awe problems if we aren't careful. How do we know if we have lost our amazement for the Lord? I think there are a few questions we could ask.

Do we *know* God is God? Do we *know* Him and not just *of* Him? Do we *marvel* at the simple fact that He is God? That He is the *"the Alpha and the Omega, the first and the last, the beginning and the end,"* according to Revelations 22:13 (ESV). Do we gaze upon His glory and *believe*, He is sovereign? Isaiah 43:11 (AMP) says, *"I, [only] I, am the Lord, And there is no Savior besides Me."* Are we *engaged* with the great "I AM"? Are we in awe? These are questions we should think about and understand the answers to.

Do we *remember* why Christ died? Christ died for the people on this earth *so that we could be free*. It is through Jesus' *death* that our broken *relationship with God* was *restored*. John 3:16 shows that we were *granted the chance*, the precious gift that needs no repayment, just an understanding, an acceptance of what the gift cost and a will wanting to believe in the One that gave that gift.

Do we *read* the Word with amazement? God wants our mouths to drop and wants us to take in His glory. *He wants us to read*, see, and know that He is the Lord, and there is no one else. Isaiah 45:6 (AMP) says, *"From the rising to the setting of the sun [the world over] there is no one except Him."*

- Genesis 1:1 (ESV) says, *"In the beginning, God created the heavens and the earth."*

- Revelation 22:20–21 (AMP) says, *"He who testifies and affirms these things says, "Yes, I am coming quickly." Amen.*

Come, Lord Jesus. The grace of the Lord Jesus (the Christ, the Messiah) be with all [the saints—all believers, those set apart for God]. Amen."

These verses alone should cause us amazement that the beginning starts with God and ends with Him, while granting victory for those who walk faithfully, believing in Him.

Do we struggle with control? As long as we try to control everything, we can't walk in amazement of something bigger. Being awestruck or amazed comes when we experience something bigger than ourselves. If we allow God to show His omnipresence and omniscience on a regular basis, then we can trust that God is in control, and the pressure is off. Matthew 10:30 (AMP) says, *"But even the very hairs of your head are all numbered [for the Father is sovereign and has complete knowledge]."* Let's release our control and look at things bigger than ourselves.

Of course, there could be more questions added to this list, but often, amazement is lost when our hearts become numb as we take God for granted. We can't keep looking for random buckets to quench our thirst when the Fountain of Living Water is there to flow through us. We can't go after our own appetites when God is saying "I am the Bread of Life." We can't ever lose our wonderment with God! Remember our glorious future—that we don't have to wait until heaven to be amazed—to know how blessed we are. John 1:14 (ESV) says, *"And the Word became flesh and dwelt among us, and we have seen his glory, glory as of the only Son from the Father, full of grace and truth."* As Christians, we remember his glory and keep a constant flow in front of us that are bigger than ourselves. When our hearts start to grovel in fear and doubt, we need to marvel in awe and wonder.

A few years back, my husband and I were able to explore a few iconic places, the Grand Canyon and Zion National Park being two of them. To say these two places were breathtaking would be an understatement. These sites encompass the word awe! While the Grand Canyon looks down as far as the eye can see, Zion looks up as far as the eye can see. Both angles capture amazement and the awesomeness of something so much more magnificent than ourselves. I visit places like this, and all I can think is God wants to make my mouth drop. He wants me to remember where it all began. Our awe begins with the Creator. He's the God of design, a God who is both intentional and purposeful, and a God who can be trusted always. In trying to capture all the different angles with my phone, trying not to miss a single thing, in the end, my camera came up short. To regain the awe that brought so much joy to my soul, I would need to go back to the very places that satisfied and filled my heart. That's how it is with God and worship. John Piper says it well, "God is most glorified in us when we are most satisfied in him."[65] With joyful submission and satisfaction, we continually come back, we continually repent of our sins, and we continually ask for new revelation as He directs our paths to the next level of amazement.

It's in these awe moments that tend to bring a breath of ease. As we take in beauty, we remember where the Lord has taken us and think about where the road will lead next. I'm reminded that every second of every day, we have the opportunity to live in the presence of the Lord, and our praise should be ready to be released high above. When the progression starts, there's nothing that can stop it, and God meets us right where we are and whispers to our attending ears as we gaze at His wonder. Fervent worshippers emerge as we open our hearts to coming back to the simple truth that God is God, having a continual adoration for the One who, according to 1 Timothy 6:15 (ESV), "*is the blessed and only Sovereign, the King of kings and Lord of lords.*"

The Silent Progression

During worship, our hearts can shift from earth to heaven in an instant. As the Holy Spirit ushers us deeper into the presence of God, we gain a clearer perspective, causing our whole hearts to block everything but Him. As mentioned, when the deep presence of the Lord takes over, the stress goes away; the fears subside, and peace fills our hearts. We sing, raise our hands, and even dance, but it's the silent moments where our mouths don't speak that the gentle whisper of the Lord breaks through. Andrew Murray says, "The very thought of God in His majesty and holiness should silence us." [66] Stillness is a time to grow in our intimacy with the Lord, and when we become silent, we can recognize His love in a whole new way.

The world is noisy, and complete silence may seem impossible, even a little awkward. We worry about filling the void of silence, but silence is exactly what we often need. My husband and I are complete opposites when it comes to personalities. He's an introvert, and I'm an extrovert. I know the agony in trying to be okay with not talking. It's tough and seems almost impossible. The silence causes me to question—to rush in and keep talking when my husband is calm and content. I guess he thinks internally, so it may not always be calm, but externally, he remains quiet. The thing is, even as an extrovert, I know I can have a quiet heart. All I have to do is be disciplined and look for ways to achieve stillness and reflection. A minute or two is all it takes to get a taste of God's goodness. When we break away from life to be still, the time multiples with the Lord naturally. I know, quiet can be hard to find. With two small boys, I find that the best time usually happens by staying up extra late just to have the silence. It does cost me sleep, but during the season I'm in, it's worth it. The silence reminds me that whatever the cost, drawing near to the Lord should be my continuous desire. It's in response to His glory that we should want to silence our voice and quiet our souls to make His voice louder. A.W. Tozer wrote, "In some instances, absolute silence might well become our greatest act of worship."[67] I want this all the time. I want to stand in absolute silence and say, "Ok, Lord, I'm listening. Speak to my heart. Bring me closer to you." No matter what goes on in life, He is still worthy to be praised and still knows what He is doing.

It's through life's tensions that the Lord has taught me about worship and how He works through a calm assurance. The striving can stop. Contentment can be found in a true worshipper. In the calm, God stirs hearts wanting to desire Him above anything else. Stillness, rest, and a quiet heart is how we find this. Psalm 131:2 (AMP) says, *"Surely I have calmed and quieted my soul; Like a weaned child [resting] with his mother, My soul is like a weaned child within me [composed and freed from discontent]."* We have to remember that worship is not about what's happening in this world, on a stage, or in a church building. It's not about how we feel things should go or about the noise around us. It's about opening our hearts to the One who deserves our praise and worship the most. The One who should get all our attention and all the glory. The heart of worship is living in wonder and amazement of the great "I Am." It's digging into scriptures and allowing the Bible to expose the heart problems that have caused our awe to diminish. The Bibles allows us to know the magnificent glory of God, His goodness, and sovereignty and prompts us to fully surrender with gladness. More than ever, we need to quietly meditate and gaze upon the glory of the Lord so we don't give way to something else. Everything is competing for our minds and hearts; therefore, our intimacy with Him should not remain idle but grow in a silent progression. Isaiah 46:10 (AMP) says, *"Be still and know (recognize, understand) that I am God. I will be exalted among the nations! I will be exalted in the earth."*

As a true worshipper, let us remember to worship with everything we have, even when that tank may feel empty.

Hold on to the truth of God's Word and allow it to be our anchor in the storm. We need to keep moving forward, keep maturing, so that the awe and wonder seep into our hearts, and allow us to see the importance of many things, including people. We look at the bigger story: the reason people matter and the reason worship brings us all together. The church is a place where we feel Him near and a place where we can gain clarity to do His will. We need to continually return as disciples for the Lord, ready to go deeper and wider for Him.

Continue Steadfastly

We all know we don't need a church building to worship the Lord. We've been reminded that our worship shouldn't stop when we leave a service and can be expressed anywhere, at any time. If this is true, then what's the big deal about church? Is it necessary? Important? Why should we go? We live in a time where church can be put on the back burner, or the main function is forgotten. The main function *is* what makes it beautiful. Church is where our reverence meets God's presence in worship. It's where people come alongside each other, maturing in the things of the Lord. It's where we grow while hearing, then live out what has transformed our hearts. In Acts 2, we see the day of Pentecost arrive and the filling of the Holy Spirit beginning His work. After Peter preached, three thousand souls were saved, and the church was born. We see what happens immediately after in Acts 2:42 (AMP). *"They were continually and faithfully devoting themselves to the instruction of the apostles, and to fellowship, to eating meals together and to prayers."* The people of Judea gave everything they had for the work of the church. They put the pedal to the medal and continued steadfastly.

Continuing steadfastly means our lives can't stop after we accept Christ. It's in discipleship that we keep growing for the rest of our lives and help as many others find the Lord along the way. Now, let's be honest: attending church can be tough at times. Neglect may very well start to creep in for many reasons: busy schedules, prefer online streaming, community challenges, laziness, or commitment issues. Maybe there is this "perfect church" mentality, and when expectations aren't met, people give up or hop around looking for it. Maybe people have been hurt by churches and never want to step foot inside one again. There are lots of reasons not to take church seriously or neglect it. The bigger questions we should ask are, *What's missing? Where do our hearts lie with the Lord? Why are we skipping church?* We should know church is not only a building but a tool to help people know and grow in Christ. As we have experienced lately, online streaming has its benefits and may very well be necessary, but we also realize the constant need for fellowship and relationship with both the Lord and people—and not only on Sunday. Overall, we have to remember when we meet as a church body, in person, it brings greater unity and strength to help our dying world. Fellowship with the church body is essential, and the Bible commands us in Hebrews 10:25 (AMP) *"not to forsake meeting together [as believers for worship and instruction], as is the habit of some, but encourage one another; and all the more [faithfully] as you see the day [of Christ's return] approaching."* The most important reason to come to church is for the world. We help the world by growing as disciples.

Another area where attending church can challenge our worship is when we are physically there but focus on ourselves or the many distractions we bring with us. Are we coming to church with a heart that has meditated on the goodness of God and is prepared even before walking through the doors? Or are we distracted? How often, if we are honest, do we come into church thinking about what we can get from a service, thinking about what God should do in our lives? The consumer attitude in the church is rampant, and I have been guilty of that as well. I find myself often reexamining whether I have a wholehearted surrender needed to glorify and admire Christ because of what I know and believe about Him. No one knows the hearts of anyone else who walks in the doors of their church, but I know for myself distraction can appear and interfere easily. We've all experienced one distraction or another:

- Rushing to church

- Arguing with your spouse

- Dropping crying kids off at the nursery

- Getting cut off in the parking lot

- Drinking coffee to cure tiredness, only to miss the beginning of service

Whatever the distraction, it's important to recognize, more than ever, that we need steady hearts that are ready, and we need hearts that are looking out for the people around us.

Whenever I escape distraction, I try to remind myself there are broken people everywhere. There are broken Christians sitting beside us, ones who have fallen into the habit of not meeting. As one body, we need to stand with each other and through prayer fight for each other. The Bible says in Hebrews 3:13 (ESV), *"Exhort one another every day, as long as it is called 'today,' that none of you may be hardened by the deceitfulness of sin."* 1 Corinthians 12:26 (ESV) says, *"If one member suffers, all suffer together; if one member is honored, all rejoice together."* We need to fight our own distractions so we can fight for others. There is nothing that can replace being with the saints of the church and the peace of knowing we are not alone in this world. The church body provides the encouragement, the prayer, the Word, and the chance to use our gifts to serve others. As we enter church with a heart fully surrendered, we can witness the love for the Lord magnifying and the love for people enhancing. We stand side by side in our brokenness, imprisonment, and pain and thank the Lord for filling our hearts with His glory. Oh, what a time to worship alongside others. A time that gives us a glimpse of heaven, the continuation and forever fellowship with our Lord. Let's not allow ourselves to go through the motions with skeptical and critical hearts but embrace the mission of Christ. Everyone is hungry for the truth, the peace, the freedom, the acceptance, and others want to escape from their prison as well. Living solitary lives will not grant us a victorious Christian life. If we want joy and peace in our hearts, we have to be faithful to the church.

We admire and worship the Lord with joyful submission because we remember the cross. That alone brings amazement, awe, and astonishment into our hearts. Why would we settle for just church when we can gaze upon His beauty, soak in His majesty, and stand in awe? There will be times when our flesh and hearts will fail, but we must remember He is our strength and our portion.[68] God fights on our behalf and rescues us from our own moments of glory. It's only His strength that pulls our hearts back to remembrance once more.

CHAPTER 9

Renewed Perspective: Eternal Hearts

Finding joy in this journey is not the whole story.

I used the phrase "find joy in the journey" often when I despaired through one of many weight loss ventures. One day at a time, one pound at a time. I needed to find strength in the Lord and joy in the challenges, or the process would never work. I continually asked, could I do this really hard thing? Did it matter? Would my joy in the journey become complete? Then, the comforting words of Jesus reminded me, "You can, it does, and it already has been!" John 17:13 (AMP) says, *"But now I am coming to You; and I say these things [while I am still] in the world so that they may experience My joy made full and complete and perfect within them [filling their hearts with My delight]."*

We The Redeemed

I knew all along my weight loss journey was about more than the end result. It was about the transformation in my heart to not only help the physical but to focus on the training that mattered—mostly my spiritual training. Finding joy in the Lord, through every season of life, is essential, but we shouldn't be too content with only this. The Bible tells us there is more to this life, and why our hearts ache for more. Yes, our joy can be made complete in Him now, but our final destination should be what we long for. Ecclesiastes 3:11 (AMP) says, *"He has made everything beautiful and appropriate in its time. He has also planted eternity [a sense of divine purpose] in the human heart [a mysterious longing which nothing under the sun can satisfy, except God]—yet man cannot find out (comprehend, grasp) what God has done (His overall plan) from the beginning to the end."*

The heart has always longed for something, and there has always been that tension that asks—Is this it? What's life all about? Why are we truly here on this earth? There has to be more. These questions I have heard countless times. Because of what Christ did on the cross, our future as followers of Jesus is eternity. Revelation 21:4 (AMP) says, *"He will wipe away every tear from their eyes; and there will no longer be death; there will no longer be sorrow and anguish, or crying, or pain; for the former order of things has passed away."*

Heaven is where Christ dwells and will be the place, one day, where we will be welcomed with open arms. Until we get there, our desire should be to live a holy life and one pleasing to God. It's this resurrected life that enables us to walk, side by side in fellowship, with the Resurrected King here on this earth. That provides our stability in life's battles.

The longing for more, for purpose, for acceptance, for calling is planted deep within us, so why is it such a battle to live redeemed? Why is it so hard to gaze up at heaven regularly? Maybe, we make things too complicated. Perhaps, we are so stuck in our ways that we prioritize our desires and wants—leaving no room for knowing or hearing from the Lord. Could it be, we are confused, so we block out the confusion with what the world tells us we should be doing and believing. As Christians, we must remember we were bought with a price.[69] Christ redeemed us from the pit, and he crowned us with steadfast love and mercy.[70] Jesus was the perfect sacrifice, holy and spotless—sacrificing his priceless blood for the forgiveness of our sins. What a Savior, what a God we have!

Now is the time to honor and glorify Him within our physical bodies. We take one step at a time, one act of obedience, at a time. Psalm 119:105 (ESV) says, *"Your word is a lamp to my feet and a light to my path."* We won't be able to see all the turns of life from afar, but God gives us enough light to see right in front of our first step. As we eagerly await our promised heavenly bodies and long for what is to come, in the meantime, we must work out our salvation all for the glory of God.

Lift Up Our Eyes

The things we do on this earth, the situations we face are greater, bigger than us. The mission for Christ was placed in our hands to go and do, to overcome. Yes, this fallen world has been decaying our bodies daily, and we are wasting away by the second. Our momentary afflictions here on earth are painfully visible. To get through this life, we need to focus on the unseen as mentioned in 2 Corinthians 4:16-18 (ESV).

Our God cannot be compared to anything or anyone. He never relaxes. He knows all and is in all things. He created the heavens and the earth and everything in it. He will create the new heavens and the new earth. God has given us the Holy Spirit, the power we need to fix our eyes on the prize and take action. Speaking of taking action, ever regret not doing something when you know God placed it on your heart to do? We wonder, *Was that really God?* Did we make it up? Then, the excuses roll around, and we end up missing out. I'm sure I've missed out on more than I can remember, but I remember one specific time.

Sitting in church, I happened to look to my left and saw a woman about my age who was pregnant. The causal eye drift happens sometimes, so I didn't think much of it. That was until the Lord pointed out the woman was my new neighbor. I thought, *Interesting!* And I decided to investigate. Sure enough, she was my neighbor, but I had no idea she attended church. As the weeks went on, I saw her sitting by herself in the same service I was attending. Mind you, we have three to choose from on Sunday mornings, so the chances were slim, but there she was. She always caught my eye, and I always picked her out of the crowd. While I felt like a stalker and a weirdo, I also felt the Lord pressing me to talk to her and offer a meal after the baby was born. The first opportunity to make a connection arrived, but I felt it wasn't the right time. Honestly, I chickened out and felt like I blew it! About eight months went by when I didn't see her at church, then eventually, I noticed her and the baby. I felt too awkward now to randomly approach a stranger, so I retreated to my house with regret, again missing out on blessing another. You see, I had forgotten to look up. I had forgotten to ask the Lord to give me the courage and strength to allow the awkwardness and walk in faith to show love. Eventually, another opportunity arose at the mailbox, and I finally introduced myself. It probably could have been different, but in the end, I learned a valuable lesson. Always look up when everything in you wants to look down and shy away.

In the Bible, Jesus even leaves us an example on how our relationship with God should be. Jesus lifted His eyes on several occasions:

- In Luke 6:20 (ESV), before ministering, He lifted his eyes: *"And he lifted up his eyes on his disciples..."*

- In John 6:5 (ESV), before miracles, He lifted his eyes: *"Lifting up his eyes, then, and seeing that a large crowd was coming toward him..."*

- In John 11:39–41 (ESV) when He raised Lazarus from the dead, the Bible says: *"And Jesus lifted up his eyes and said, 'Father, I thank you that you have heard me.'"*

- In John 17:1 (ESV), before prayer, Jesus lifted his eyes: *"He lifted up his eyes to heaven and said..."*

By lifting our eyes like Jesus, we can remember with gratitude our relationship with Him:

- We remember the gospel in Psalm 103:11–12 (AMP): *"For as the heavens are high above the earth, so great is His lovingkindness toward those who fear and worship Him [with awe-filled respect and deepest reverence], As far as the east is from the west, so far has He removed our transgressions from us."*

- We remember our journeys in Psalm 77:11 (ESV): *"I will remember the deeds of the Lord; yes, I will remember your wonders of old."*

- We remember the present in 1 Chronicles 16:11 (ESV): *"Seek the Lord and his strength; seek his presence continually!"*

Each day grants us an opportunity to lift our eyes. According to Psalm 29:2 (ESV), with an eternal perspective, we *"ascribe to the Lord the glory due his name; worship the Lord in the splendor of holiness."* We thank Him for all we have and all He has done. We know that His love reaches to the heavens, His faithfulness stretches to the sky, His righteousness is like a mighty mountain, and His justice like the oceans deep.[71] It's with eternity in mind that we become anchored and remain established in the One that brings hope to all.

Anchored Hope

Philippians 3:20–21 (ESV) says:

> *"But our citizenship is in heaven, and from it we await a Savior, the Lord Jesus Christ, who will transform our lowly body to be like his glorious body, by the power that enables him even to subject all things to himself."*

Where is our hope? Have we put it away, or did we wake up from our slumber to remember this earth is not our home? Heaven is going to be awesome, but too often, we fear missing out on what is left behind (like I've mentioned from my own fears). Some may also fear heaven won't live up to par. The hard truth, the truth that can scare a lot of people, even faith fearing Christians, is that one-day, this life will come to an end. One day, we will come face to face with Jesus. I tremble at the thought. Not in a scary way but in a "what is it going to be like" kind of way. Immediately, my mind goes to the song *"I can only Imagine,"* by MercyMe. It has been played millions of times, and I'm sure a lot of us know the song, but do we ever go back to these songs and really listen to the words? There's a reason this song has touched so many hearts around the world.

To one day have our gaze transfixed on Jesus's face is a thought that should bring us to tears when we really let it sink in. Let it sink in now—it's okay. Take a minute and think about gazing upon the beauty of the Lord and beholding His face. Oh, what a sight that will be! Sure, heaven can seem hard to grasp, but the Bible gives us hope that there is a place far beyond what we can imagine. There will be mansions and streets made out of gold. There will be perfect weather, and darkness will be no more; we will be illuminated by God's presence, by the glory of God. There will be total joy, no sadness, no regrets, no sickness, no poverty; all the tears will be wiped away. There will be no unrighteousness. There will be worship and praise going on forever as we sing around the throne of God. We will recognize our family and friends, and there will be continual fellowship with God and with all the saints from the old to new testament. Oh, what a place to call home! [72]

Heaven will not be a dull, drab, or boring place but a place where righteousness dwells.[73] Why would we be so excited to share what Christ has to offer if this world ends with a failed promise? Heaven is redemption in full form. No more sin, and no more death—the perfect promise for us to rest on forever. There was a popular picture floating around awhile back that really stopped me in my tracks, and immediately, I pictured what heaven could be like. In the picture, there is a woman embracing Jesus. It's almost as if the minute she saw Him, she ran as fast as she could and jumped into His warm embrace. Then, you see her face. It says it all. She made it! She was finally in the arms of Jesus forever. Oh, what a relief to finally be home. The title of the picture is *First Day in Heaven Painting—I HELD HIM and Would Not Let Him Go.* [74]

Knowing there is something more glorious than earth, we can't be too quick to forget. Let's not bury it with idols of this earth. Compared to eternity, we should ask ourselves regularly if what we are doing is worth it. We should remind ourselves the pain we feel now will be wiped away. Can we trust in this hope that anchors our souls? Hebrews 6:19 (AMP) says, *"This hope [this confident assurance] we have as an anchor of the soul [it cannot slip and it cannot break down under whatever pressure bears upon it]—a safe and steadfast hope that enters within the veil [of the heavenly temple, that most Holy Place in which the very presence of God dwells]."*

Eternity Starts Now

Colossians 1:27 (AMP) says, *"God [in His eternal plan] chose to make known to them how great for the Gentiles are the riches of the glory of this mystery, which is Christ in and among you, the hope and guarantee of [realizing the] glory."* Because we indwell with Christ, we can look forward to sharing His glory.[75] Hope doesn't start when we get to heaven but the very second we accept Jesus as our Lord and Savior. We have unity with Christ, which means we have authority, power, and the ability to receive all His promises now. Let's not miss out on what we have here on earth. We mustn't fall asleep but be awake and alert, allowing Christ to shine on us. We must look carefully at our walks with God and chose the best use of our time. Ephesians 5:14 (AMP) says, *"For this reason He says, 'Awake, sleeper, And arise from the dead, And Christ will shine [as dawn] upon you and give you light.'"*

The days are evil, so we must move with urgency. Like Peter, will we jump out of the boat without hesitation when we see Jesus?[76] Do we live with the urgency that Christ could come back any minute? Revelation 22:7 (AMP) says, *"And behold, I am coming quickly. Blessed (happy, prosperous, to be admired) is the one who heeds and takes to heart and remembers the words of the prophecy [that is, the predictions, consolations, and warnings] contained in this book (scroll)."* The assurance of heaven should not cause us to settle into idle living but propel us to live with expectancy. To know that we will all give an account for what we have done on this earth should shift our perspective. We perk up to the fact that a holy lifestyle matters. What we do with our time matters. How we respond to trials matter. We must choose not to get stuck in frivolous activities or the momentary, yet painful afflictions.

There are many stories in the Bible of people who, at one point or another, lost sight of what mattered most. Luke 10:38–42 shows us two sisters, one who sat at Jesus' feet and the other distracted, anxious, and troubled by many things. What was the only thing needed? Listening to Jesus.

Then, we see Peter, a man who once again didn't understand his changed life. He had been restored after denying Jesus and now was given the actual blueprints to what God had in store for him. What did Peter do? According to John 21:21 (AMP), he asked, *"Lord, and what about this man [what is in his future]?"* Ever notice how he referred to John as "this man?" You get the sense that Peter had some hidden grudge against John, and maybe a little jealousy or comparison snuck in there too. Nonetheless, instead of marveling that God's plan for His life was right in front of his face, he decided not to hear in the moment. His focus was on someone else. How often do we do this? We focus on what God is calling someone else to do and forget what He has placed in front of us. We remember Jesus's response in John 21:22 (AMP), *"If I want him to stay alive until I come [again], what is that to you? You follow Me!"* Basically, He's saying it's none of your business, Peter. Let's get on with the show!

What we can learn from these two scenarios is that anything can get in the way. Anything can distract us from lifting our eyes or seeing God's path. He will show us, but we must be willing to keep our eyes fixed toward God so our hearts and tongues consistently rejoice in Him. Psalm 16:11 (ESV) says, *"You make known to me the path of life; in your presence there is fullness of joy; at your right hand are pleasures forevermore."* When we look forward, we see earthly sorrow ending, and all the pain is finally wiped away. There will be infinite joy and everlasting happiness.

We have so much to look forward to: to meet the men and women of faith, to ask all the questions, to join hands with each other, to always see God high and lifted up, and to finally be able to worship Jesus with nothing competing for our hearts. The Bible says in Romans 5:2 (AMP), *"Let us rejoice in our hope and the confident assurance of [experiencing and enjoying] the glory of [our great] God [the manifestation of His excellence and power]."* The day we see Jesus face to face will come, but while we wait, let's keep holding onto the promises that never fail. We are nearing home, but we aren't there yet.

CHAPTER 10

Treasured Perseverance: Passionate Hearts

"**I** can't believe she died."

As I held the crinkled newspaper in my hand, a newspaper that I never stop to read, I asked myself why I read it today. Why this moment? As I sat alone in a house I shared with my college friends, I wept for what I did and didn't know. Sara was the first person I shared Christ's love with, the first person God showed me why He wants me to be passionate for Him.

It's been fourteen years, and not a day goes by when I don't think about this beautiful person God had put into my life. I look at the timeline, and I can't help but feel goosebumps rise when I think about the purpose God places in our lives. He placed Sara in my life on purpose and for a purpose, but sometimes, the answers don't come right away or on this side of eternity. You see, the reason this hurt was because I never witnessed her transformation in Christ. I shared the truth with

Sara, gave her a Bible, and was her friend, yet one semester later, she died in a tragic car crash.

That empty seat in economics class continually reminded me why I never want to lose my passion for the Lord and people. I never want my heart to give up. I never want to miss that one person who needs hope—who needs a friend—who needs a listening ear. That one person who needs the only One we will ever need in this life and the next: Jesus Christ.

I still don't know all the answers. I don't know if Sara accepted the Lord before she died. What I do know is that we serve a God vastly bigger than any of us can imagine. I know she had a chance to hear the gospel, and I have to leave the rest to God. Passion and calling means so much more to me now than it did then. No one on this earth was created by accident but on purpose and for a purpose. There's no afterthought with God, only the full-fledged plan and perfect design. He knows our lives beginning to end, and it's our job to stay focused, passionate for Him, and put away anything that distracts us from blessing someone else and touching their lives with God's love.

Easily Passionate, Wrongly Passionate

No one has to make us be passionate about something. Usually, when something occurs in our lives that is unexpected or that brings a sense of thrill or excitement, passion magically appears without much effort. While passion is not all bad, I do wonder if we, as Christ followers, give more emphasis to *what* we are passionate about rather than *who* we are passionate about. All the accomplishments, the status, all we attain through religious effort, or anything else in our lives that dominates are pulling at us. Do we want more of those things? Why do we want them? Will we throw them away to know Christ more and know Him well?

I'm reminded of 1 Peter 2:11–12 (ESV): *"Beloved, I urge you as sojourners and exiles to abstain from the passions of the flesh, which wage war against your soul. Keep your conduct among the Gentiles honorable, so that when they speak against you as evildoers, they may see your good deeds and glorify God on the day of visitation."* This warning shows how destructive fleshly passions can be. How do we know? They wage war against our souls. They cause us to stand no longer in awe and in reverence of the Lord. We have all been in slumps and can all recognize when the light of Christ starts to dim in our lives. It's when other things seem brighter than Christ that we are stripped of longing to do the very thing He created us to do. Passion creates devotion, and whenever devotion increases, it can either mature us or cause us to crash, leaving us helpless and struggling to find our identity once more. However, if we look back on a couple verses we can see exactly who we are. In 1 Peter 2:9–10 (ESV), the Bible says, *"But you are a chosen race, a royal priesthood, a holy nation, a people for his own possession, that you may proclaim the excellencies of him who called you out of darkness into his marvelous light. Once you were not a people, but now you are God's people; once you had not received mercy, but now you have received mercy."*

Knowing who we are, that we are God's chosen possession, should help us to act with confidence. We all struggle. We all come up short. When we slip, we can recover. We need to fight off our own sins, fight against our earthly desires, and try not to gain perfection; we remember that *"the steps of a good man are ordered by the Lord,"* according to Psalm 37:23 (NKJV). He has brought us out of the darkness and into the marvelous light. Our souls were made to proclaim His excellencies, and we should be thrilled and excited to do just that. Because our purpose and passion shape what we do, how we lead, and who we influence, we have to ask: How do we preserve the reason for which we were created? We replace fleshly desires with Godly ones by praying, fasting, and meditating on the Word of God. Just like Paul, we keep our passions and desires under control.[77] All of us have the ability to say no to sin. We can know who we are, but more importantly, we find our calling and passion when we realize God's ultimate design for the universe.

The Grand Purpose

I remember a time I constantly prayed for more discipline. For years when my Bible study met, that was the prayer at the top of my list. I would continue to pray for this and ask for prayer from others, yet nothing ever changed. I wanted to be more disciplined in reading my Bible, as well as other areas of my life. Looking back now, I see the problem. The problem wasn't *praying* for discipline but actually *taking action* and *applying* discipline to my life. As a result, I became confused and annoyed with my life, and the focus became about me. As you might remember from a previous chapter, I wrestled with sayings like, "God was going to use me in a big way" and that "I couldn't wait for him to use me" and that "I could feel my purpose coming." There are a lot of me's and I's in there, don't you think? It was eating me up inside, trying to figure out what God had planned. Then, I realized something. I realized I had missed the point entirely. The number one thing we need in this life is to radiate to the world how magnificent Jesus is and give Him all the glory in everything! That was it. That's where I lost sight. I was so focused on how God was going to *use* me, thinking things were going to fall into my lap, that I ended up not taking any action at all. I was wandering in the abyss with a "woe is me" attitude and had wasted precious time.

The point of the Christian life is to magnify the Lord, to radiate His love to those around us. But we can't do that if we forget His greatness or haven't met with Him in a while. Our first priority should be to ask the Lord to open our hearts, that they be flooded with light by the Holy Spirit so we know and cherish the hope to which He has called us.[78] The more we recognize how powerful and mighty God is, the more we allow Him to look as big as He really is. He is already grand, already high and lifted up. We just need to act like He is. I had to come to terms and not allow excuses to get in the way of obedience. Through action, thought, and heart, we are to proclaim His excellencies. This is why we are saved; this is why we need His Word to invade all parts of our lives. We were made to make Christ look magnificent.

Isaiah 40:28 (ESV):

"Have you not known? Have you not heard? The Lord is the everlasting God, the Creator of the ends of the earth. He does not faint or grow weary; his understanding is unsearchable."

Isaiah 45:5–7 (ESV):

"I am the Lord, and there is no other, besides me there is no God; I equip you, though you do not know me, that people may know, from the rising of the sun and from the west, that there is none besides me; I am the Lord, and there is no other. I form light and create darkness; I make well-being and create calamity; I am the Lord, who does all these things."

Psalm 147:3–5 (ESV):

"He heals the brokenhearted and binds up their wounds. He determines the number of the stars; he gives to all of them their names. Great is our Lord, and abundant in power; his understanding is beyond measure."

1 Timothy 6:15–16 (ESV):

"...he who is the blessed and only Sovereign, the King of kings and Lord of lords, who alone has immortality, who dwells in unapproachable light, whom no one has ever seen or can see. To him be honor and eternal dominion. Amen."

We have a big God, and He has a purpose—a grand design. We are to be light in the world, not as lamps, hidden under a basket, waiting to be placed on a stand.[79] We take action, letting our light shine before men. The way we do that is through obedience, faithfulness, and calling.

Calling All Strengths

Besides knowing and loving God, we all want to know our life's purpose. What is our calling? What does calling really mean? It seems the word *calling* often floats around without landing on specific assignments. I won't judge or assume about other's callings, but since I was confused and frustrated to know my life's purpose, I needed to understand what being called actually meant. *Can we really do anything we put our minds to?* Does practice really make perfect? We hear these words and think, *I can do anything* yet end up doing nothing. Or we strive so hard for something that ends up not working out, no matter how many times we try. *Why is that?* Why is it so hard to figure this out? The Greek word for *called* comes from the root word, *Kaleo*, which means to summon, to invite, to call aloud and to call forth.[80] As Christians, the minute we are born again, God has a specific invitation addressed to each of us. When we receive and accept that specific invite, we are then able to accomplish the work He desires for us to do on this earth. We can take a peek at someone else's invitation and try to replicate it, but we won't get very far with it. Too often, we tend to build on our weaknesses, thinking they are strengths. It's when we operate in our strengths that purpose comes to life.

The idea that we can't do everything can make us feel inferior, can't it? I know I've felt this. We say, "I wish I could do that or have that ministry, or I wish God thought as highly of me as he does her." These thoughts have come, but I realize (once again) that I can't do everything, and whatever God called me to do is not about me. Our calling is about what God has specifically given us and how He wants it to be used to help others. We can find joy in our callings. God does give us the desires of our hearts, but the purpose is to glorify the Lord. I'm reminded of David. This guy failed so many times, yet he was willing to admit his weaknesses and truly knew where God gifted him in life. He was able to remain content, remembering that the body of Christ is a team effort.

Psalm 131:1–2 (AMP) says:

> *Lord, my heart is not proud, nor my eyes haughty;*
> *Nor do I involve myself in great matters,*
> *Or in things too difficult for me.*
> *Surely I have calmed and quieted my soul;*
> *Like a weaned child [resting] with his mother,*
> *My soul is like a weaned child within me [composed and*
> *freed from discontent].*

So, how do we find our strengths and the call God has for us? This is tricky because we all experience things differently, yet throughout the Bible, we can see what faithful people did when called.

The first thing we see is prayer. Praying for direction, for a clear sign, for the next step is a nonnegotiable action. We need to start asking the Lord for a yearning not only for Him but for other people. We need to ask Him to show us the steps we should take. The Lord even places people in our lives to confirm this as well. Recently, I reflected on my life to see if God had been revealing my strengths and gifts without me realizing it. Sure enough, He had. People have helped me see what my strengths are. I received letters from people that expressed what they admired about my character and emails from friends who saw where I showed confidence or operated well. Sometimes, I even asked for honest reviews, and it was worth it. Finally understanding my strengths has helped me gain confidence in what God is calling me to do. Along with people helping me, there were life experiences that also assisted in the shaping process. Looking back on missions trips and service opportunities, I realized what I was good at and what I wasn't. The cool thing was the things that lit a fire in my heart were the same things people had confirmed as my strengths. It took many years to come to the realization that I'm actually gifted with strengths and how I can contribute to the body of Christ. My process is still being refined, but each step of obedience leads me to where Christ wants me to be—faithful.

Faithfulness is the key to our calling. When we are faithful, when we dedicate everything we have and everything we are to the Lord and hold nothing back, that's when everything starts making a bit more sense—as the pieces start coming together. God wants to see our faithfulness—especially in the midst of the waiting. Moses, David, and Paul come to mind. Their journeys were all lifelong journeys of continual trust and obedience. However, I'm also reminded of Elijah and Elisha and how Elisha's faithfulness stood out. There came a time when Elijah was no longer fit to lead after his "woe is me" attitude would not subside. Therefore, the Lord said to go find this young farmer boy who would finish what he wouldn't. From the moment Elijah placed his cloak on Elisha, signifying God's call, Elisha was faithful day after day, year after year, until it was time. The many years of faithful serving built Elisha's character and stabilized him so he could wisely step into the call God gave him. But he had to serve and wait. We read this story in 1-2 Kings and see that God wants faithfulness to be our way of life. If we can't remain faithful, how are we ever able to work out our calling? I love this quote by Mother Teresa: *"I do not pray for success, I ask for faithfulness."* [81] This is exactly where *we* should be—faithful until God says it's time.

God is always stirring in our hearts. He is always pursuing us and wanting us to look past ourselves to gaze at the whole picture. Our calling is only from God, and we work out our calling right where we are. What has God already put in your hand that you can accomplish whole-heartedly right now? Too often, we want the big, bold, exciting call, yet we must find God in the midst of where we are currently. We can't wait for "one day when" because we aren't promised tomorrow. Now is when we should say, "Lord, help us surrender early and completely. Lord, help us take each day as a gift to cultivate our passion for you and allow you to work through us." We find our strengths by asking a close friend what they see in us. We start somewhere—serving in our local churches, figuring out what comes naturally, and what makes us excited to keep going. *And* we remain faithful so God can strengthen our foundation in Him. Each step matters, and by keeping a pure heart, we will be able to begin the process, lead with excellence, and finish well.

How We Finish

Ecclesiastes 3:1–2, 6 (ESV) says, *"For everything there is a season, and a time for every matter under heaven: a time to be born, and a time to die; a time to plant, and a time to pluck up what is planted;"* ....v6, *"a time to seek, and a time to lose; a time to keep, and a time to cast away."* Seasons come, and seasons go, and when they end, where do we stand? Do we have what it takes to do whatever it takes for the Lord? Or do we give up? The ending of seasons can be hurtful and confusing, but they can also be hopeful and rewarding. They usually put our heart on display by showing us what needs to be mended and refined. Ultimately, though, seasons should always bring us closer to Jesus. That should be our goal. Each season touches the lives of people, good and bad, but hopefully, we are living in a way that glorifies the Lord with a lasting impression, not a sour note.

Do we ever stop to think about the testimony we pass on? People are always watching or observing our actions and attitudes. What do we want our lives to say? Awhile back, I remember reading a book called *Living Forward*, and in this book, they challenged people to really think about their life plan and living on purpose. They asked questions like "where do we want to end up?" They asked, What's the legacy we want to leave?" "Will it be one of intention and joy or one filled with regrets and sorrow?"[82] It sounded like a straightforward approach to examining life until they suggested people write their own eulogy. I thought that was a bit morbid as I'm actually writing it out, but for some reason, I completed the exercise. I went back through my life examining how seasons ended and new ones began. I remember feeling great joy but also feelings of regret too. There were moments I sat back and sobbed. It was great for my soul. The exercise took some time to complete, but when finished, I could read through what my heart and head already engaged in. In the end, when my time comes to go home, all I want is for people to remember that I loved Jesus with all my heart, mind, and soul. I want people to remember that I took the time to love them, that I showed compassion, that I actually lived a life that shined for the Lord. I want people to know I loved my family and prayed fervently for everyone that entered my life. I also wanted to be remembered for my hilarious jokes, but I knew that was probably a stretch.

This exercise brought to the surface so many things, so many areas I had drifted through that I didn't want to drift through any longer. Most of all, it reminded me how short life is. How each moment counts as none of us know the time when we will head home.[83] The vision matters, people matter, and the influence we have now, as well as the legacy we leave behind, matters. Just because we are moving toward home doesn't mean we give up. Instead, we look up and out on all the souls God still wants to know Him. It's the legacy we leave for the next generation, the obedient steps that help raise someone up in the Lord. Having health and wealth in this life is fleeting. It's the impact we leave on someone else's heart that could change them forever. I think of Jesus and how He only had three years in His public ministry, but those three years changed so many hearts. So many people gained hope; they gained life. As Jesus made it His prayer to finish his work, we should as well.[84]

If we are followers of Christ, we should be the most passionate people on the earth, having the Holy Spirit within us. We have the opportunity to inspire and encourage those around us. We have the privilege to cheer on the person beside us as they work out their passion and gifts that God gave. We need to be ready, not only to act in our callings but be ready to count the costs, to live in a way that shows life and faith, making Jesus the focal point. We need to be ready to finish well! I'm reminded of Caleb. As old age crept in, he never lost sight of the vision—maintaining a lifelong passion and purpose until the very end. Joshua 14:14 (NLT) says, *"he wholeheartedly followed the Lord, the God of Israel."* Caleb was a man who embraced God's promises and knew what it meant to not give up. He was a man that understood and believed that God always meant what He said. Like Caleb, let's have our ultimate passion be following the Lord wholeheartedly until the day He takes us home.

It takes an established heart to fulfill God's purpose, and it takes that same heart to finish well. God's promises breed passion, and we should embrace them daily, knowing that in the end, Jesus becomes more and more as we become less and less.[85]

Part Two
Reflections for the Heart
Chapters 6–10

Review: We see our assurance in Christ produces the type of transformation that welcomes the urgency to change. We don't stop living for Jesus the second we receive Him but continue steadfastly for the rest of our lives. We all have a choice to make. Will we become soft toward others, true worshippers, eternally focused and passionate for the things of God? Or will we remain flatfooted, unwilling to walk in obedience? Jesus takes notice of our struggles. In the midst of the battle, He knows our pains and temptations that run deep and never leaves us to fight alone. Instead, He picks up the broken pieces, gives His power and strength through healing, and shows how magnificent and loving He is.

Coming up: As we look forward, we see why our hearts need someone to love us enough to die such a costly death. We see God's holiness in a way that allows His glory to be displayed. As amazement re-enters our hearts, we stop to make sure we remain established in Jesus. Our new hearts need to be active, ready to take on purpose, and to know God's promises for the future as well as for today.

Discussion Questions

- Do you have the mindset of Christ? Do you follow His example but also recognize that He is more than an example? How do you do this?

- Do you radically put sin to death in your life, or do you allow sin to disillusion your senses? What is the pattern of attack on your life, and how does the enemy lie to you? Do you know this?

- Do you really love people or just say you do? If we could foresee all the things others would do or say to you, but couldn't do anything about, would you still love them? How should you be loving people better? Is it a priority in your life to love well? Are you willing to forgive as Jesus forgave?

- Do you understand what it means to worship? What do you worship? Do you worship out of reverence for Jesus or getting something back in return? Have you lost your wonderment of God? When was the last time you were completely still before the Lord? Are you distracted with things of this world to see the need for stillness?

- Do you lift your eyes and see heaven as the joy set before you? When you think about finally seeing Jesus face to face, what goes through your mind? Are you excited for what is promised after you die? Are you ready to meet your maker?

- Do you love the world more than God and people? What motivates you in life, and can you say that motivation leads to giving Glory to God? Do you know what you are called to do? If not, are you praying and being faithful in the waiting? How seriously do you take training up the next generation? What legacy will you leave behind?

PART 3

Established

CHAPTER 11

What's Already Been Said: God's Heart and His Promises

God is good. He knows what He is doing. When you can't trace His hand, trust His heart.

—Max Lucado, *Grace for the Moment*

Does God really know what He's doing? Can we trust His heart and hold onto His promises with assurance and hope? Do we know what His promises are? Awhile back, I had a hair appointment with my awesome stylist and couldn't wait to check out her new location or enjoy the time to catch up. Living in the same area all my life, I knew which roads would be faster and how long it should take to arrive. However, I still used my GPS, just in case. Then, the GPS voice prompted me to make a turn I knew was not the fastest way. Quickly, I hit ignore, and onward I continued. Another prompt came, telling me to take another turn off-track, and yet again, I ignored it, thinking my GPS had no clue. It turns out, the GPS offered me two chances, and I blew it. While I thought I knew best, I was the one who had no clue. The road I traveled shut down right before the turn I needed to take. A major gas leak had me scrambling to find a way back to the original GPS detour. The directions were there, the prompting was there, and if I had only listened or realized there was a reason for the detour, then I would've saved myself more stress. I wouldn't have gotten stuck, rushing to find a way back to the alternate road to freedom.

God's provisions and logistics are perfect. No, my GPS is not perfect, but it did *try* to help guide me around my own way, and this time, it had a better solution. I couldn't see the whole picture and needed help. Another funny thing I thought about was, why did I turn it on to begin with if I was so confident in my ability to find the building?

We have the tools to communicate with the main traffic coordinator. We have power from the Holy Spirit to grab every last promise and tuck them deep within our hearts. God sees the whole picture but wants us to accept and believe He means what he says. The Bible says in 2 Corinthians 1:20 (ESV), *"For all the promises of God find their Yes in him. That is why it is through him that we utter our Amen to God for his glory."* We have the means to push past discouragement, fear, brokenness, and exhaustion. However, if we are disobedient, give up too soon, or lose courage, then most likely the tools He has given weren't being used to begin with. So, I repeat these questions for all of us. *Can we fully trust that God knows what He is doing? Do we know His promises and allow them to keep us established in Him?* We find our strength and victory when we take up the sword of the Spirit. We have to understand who our God is and remember who He is from beginning to end.

Our God

It's sometimes hard to see that God actually understands what we go through or even cares, yet He does. He knows exactly what it feels like to be bombarded by weakness and temptations and understands the inner tensions from it all. Hebrews 4:15–16 (AMP) says:

> For we do not have a High Priest who is unable to sympathize and understand our weaknesses and temptations, but One who has been tempted [knowing exactly how it feels to be human] in every respect as we are, yet without [committing any] sin. Therefore let us [with privilege] approach the throne of grace [that is, the throne of God's gracious favor] with confidence and without fear, so that we may receive mercy [for our failures] and find [His amazing] grace to help in time of need [an appropriate blessing, coming just at the right moment].

Although Christ never wavered, we do. Therefore, we need His promises to pull us back to where our hearts can be anchored more securely. Because the many tensions tend to weaken our souls, we need Him to remain our rock and our firm foundation. With complete surrender, Christ will restore and transform us, allowing His love to find us in new ways. According to Romans 5:5 (AMP), *"Such hope [in God's promises] never disappoints us, because God's love has been so abundantly poured out within our hearts through the Holy Spirit who was given to us."*

It was on the cross where true love was demonstrated. It was the place where God's heart was revealed, where freedom was given as a gift, and privileges were gained for the undeserving. Romans 5:8 (AMP) says, *"But God clearly shows and proves His own love for us, by the fact that while we were still sinners, Christ died for us."* We are able to see the love of Christ so openly, yet so many of us still fall prey to forgetting the depth of that love being displayed daily. That demonstration of love was the plan all along. It was grace and mercy paving a way to remove the separation forever so none would perish. Christ's love for us is visible. It can be seen abundantly through the Word of God. Yet it's our true love for Him that is invisible to everyone but Him. So ask yourself: *How much do I really love Jesus?* How often do we allow ourselves to marvel at the cross, to see above our circumstances and the many trials of this world? When we fully marvel at the love He willingly gave us, that's when hearts turn. They not only overflow and become more visible to others, but they display the master-piece of who God is.

Revelation 21:3 (ESV) says, *"And I heard a loud voice from the throne saying, "Behold, the dwelling place of God is with man. He will dwell with them, and they will be his people, and God himself will be with them as their God."* This is why Christ wanted to save us, and this one promise should make our souls come alive. He wants to be our God! Charles Spurgeon wrote, "This is the masterpiece of all the promises; its enjoy-ment makes a heaven below and will make a heaven above. Dwell in the light of your Lord, and let your soul be always ravished with His love. Get out the marrow and fatness that this portion yields you. Live up to your privileges, and rejoice with unspeakable joy."[86] This is the masterpiece, isn't it? We have a God that is ours, and we are His. Yes, He is our God now but not in the way He will be. One day, we will see Jesus face to face, but more excitingly, we will be more intimately joined than we have ever been here on this earth.

I don't know about you, but I think Bob Ross always showed how to turn a blank canvas into a masterpiece. There's something soothing in watching him create on canvas what's swirling inside his head. In the beginning, you think, *Okay, this sounds like a good idea for a painting*, but then he starts. As he goes along, you wonder if he really knows what he's doing.

Watching him whack the brushes in between strokes, you sit in anticipation, waiting to see his vision come to life. While squinting and wondering what in the world that stroke was, our eyes eventually see it come alive. The beauty with every stroke is taking form. It becomes the masterpiece we hoped from the very beginning. The same is true for us, like the Bible says in Ephesians 2:10 (AMP), *"For we are His workmanship [His own master work, a work of art], created in Christ Jesus [reborn from above—spiritually transformed, renewed, ready to be used] for good works, which God prepared [for us] beforehand [taking paths which He set], so that we would walk in them [living the good life which He prearranged and made ready for us]."* With joy, let's live up to our privileges. Let's know what our God has promised and keep them tucked in our hearts. We not only tuck these promises in our hearts, but we study them, believe them, and act on them daily.[87] This is where we see the Promise Maker become visible. Where we can raise a banner of victory in Him with great joy.[88]

Promise Maker Promise Keeper

The Promise Maker takes our callous, broken, fearful, discouraged, and divided hearts and rejuvenates, refreshes, and restores them to something greater. Luke 1:37 (AMP) says, *"For with God nothing [is or ever] shall be impossible."* And in Isaiah 55:11 (NLT), the Lord says, *"It is the same with my word. I send it out, and it always produces fruit. It will accomplish all I want it to, and it will prosper everywhere I send it."* This is why we can hold on tight to the secure truth. Even when our hearts are in trouble, Jesus provides all we need to combat the lies and heal the pain that can enter so quick and deep. This is how we can discover the hidden battlegrounds of our hearts and how we remain established in Him.

- ***How do we gain a soft heart?*** We look at what is calloused and what has become a little too hard to resemble the love Christ wants us to share with others. We change our focus. What do we truly desire? Is it the Lord? Or have we allowed our own desires to get in the way of what Jesus is trying to teach us? A soft heart loves God and loves others, even when it's hard. It remembers unity is what makes us fully functional for Christ.

- ***How do we become a true worshiper?*** We know what's alluring us, what's causing us to be in danger of the flesh. And we flee even when we might not want to. When the illusions in life tempt us to take a step away from Jesus, we should stop and immediately run to the foot of the cross. We should kill anything that tries to steal our devotion from God and regain our senses by feasting on Him in faith. A true worshiper understands that sin can hinder our walks. But a silent progression of being in His presence causes us to be amazed. Our eyes open, and our mouths drop when we read our Bibles. Knowing our lifeline is at stake, we guard it with everything we have and keep moving forward with urgency.

- ***How do we live with an eternal heart?*** We lift our eyes. In the midst of brokenness, we see the joy set before us. We remember that although we almost didn't make it through the trial, Christ was there and is good all the time. We don't put away our hope but keep it securely anchored in the One who brings hope. An eternal heart knows unity with Christ can begin now, and as we long for heaven, we never get over the gospel. The good news is still turning hearts daily, supplying grace to desperate sinners. We may fall during this life, but we can rise again. Jesus is always in the business of giving light so we can experience His glory.

- *How do we ignite passionate hearts?* We remember what matters most in the midst of discouragement. Though we change and people around us change, our God never changes. As we stand on the rock that firmly holds us up with confidence, we know who we are in Him. A passionate heart yearns to know God and desires to share Him with others. As we learn to pray continuously, we wait faithfully for Him to reveal the steps we need to take. We know that until our heart stops beating, we are still in the race. What will we leave for the next generation? It's not how we start but how we finish, fighting to the very end.

The battles of our hearts must be kept in perspective. We remember that although there may be a problem, there is always a solution with God. In 1 Corinthians 1:9 (AMP), the Bible says, *"God is faithful [He is reliable, trustworthy and ever true to His promise—He can be depended on], and through Him you were called into fellowship with His Son, Jesus Christ our Lord."* His promises give us confidence, not only in God's ability to come through but in our ability to fully trust in Him. We will never be able to remain established in the Lord if we try to figure out life on our own, which is why we rest in His faithfulness. As we do this, our hearts begin to change, our faith strengthens, and we realize how change can make a difference in the long run.

Faithful Resting

True rest and confidence is not found in our understanding and knowledge but in trusting the One who already has it figured out. Nothing takes the Lord by surprise, and nothing will ever make Him change His mind on how much He loves us.[89] Faithful resting means we enter into God's rest. We take hold of the truth in His Word and lie our heads down on the pillow of peace.

I'm reminded of the disciples once again. In Mark chapter four we see a furious storm approached and seemed like they were all going to die, yet Jesus was there, lying peacefully on a pillow, fast asleep. The disciples freaked out. They asked if Jesus cared, and their unbelief rose to the surface. What they missed was crucial. They missed what Jesus had said before the storm came. According to Mark 4:35 (ESV), He said, *"Let us go across to the other side."* He didn't say some will go; He didn't say maybe; He said what He meant. They were all going to the other side of Galilee, and He was going to be with them. God's authority and power were present in Jesus. He cared, and He was right there in the midst of the storm. He was resting on peace.[90]

It is so easy to miss a promise, to miss what has already been said from the Lord. That's why it's important to hear His voice. We hear His voice by reading the Word. We can freak out the minute a storm starts to brew and can start to wonder if God cares, but we shouldn't act like the disciples. When we hear from God, it doesn't mean the storm is not going to be there. It simply means we have something to hold onto when the wind and waves are trying to swamp the boat. We rest on God's Word because we know it brings deliverance. The Lord is with us and will get us through to the very end.

A person who rested on a promise was Peter. While held in prison by King Herod waiting to be killed, we see Peter sleeping. He wasn't pacing back and forth pleading with God to save him. He wasn't asking, "Why, God? Why?" trying to figure out a solution. Instead, he slept peacefully on the ground, bound up in chains between two guards. What? How was he able to do this? If we take a look back, we see why he had such peace. Jesus already told Peter how he would die; therefore, Peter was able to rest because he remembered what Christ told Him.[91] It wasn't his time to die, and sure enough, an angel came to bail Peter out. Sometimes, I just sit and stare at stories like this and think to myself, *Why am I so afraid? Why can't I fully rest at times?* It's not that I'm not supposed to care about things, it's that I'm not supposed to worry. But, I still worry. In Philippians 4:6 (ESV), God says, *"Do not be anxious about anything, but in everything by prayer and supplication with thanksgiving let your requests be made known to God."* I don't know about you, but I see the words, *anything and everything,* and think, *Are you kidding me, God? How do you expect me to do this?* Then, I'm reminded it's not what He expects me to do, it's what He instructs me to do. God wants us to remain in His rest, and He wants us to have no fear; to fully trust. Why would He fail us? I find the more I go over the promises of God, the more I keep them in my mind and heart, the more peace I receive.

By drawing closer to God through prayer and the study of His Word, we become people who know the promises of God and know what kind of faith He marvels at. We don't lose hope when a storm hits but remember peace is there in the boat with us. Just like Peter, let's have the kind of peace that knows where we are and rests in what God proclaimed. The way to a God-powered and fulfilled life is through holiness in Jesus. We can have that life in Him—we just need to know how our hearts should be operating. Hearts are becoming reestablished as we speak.

CHAPTER 12

Soak It In, Live It Out: Our New Hearts

There's so much more!

I remember saying this to myself as tears ran down my face looking around at the 16,000 people singing inside a huge exhibition center. There were 127 countries represented, and stories were shared while songs were sung to testify to the oneness we all had in Christ. Some people risked their lives to share their testimonies—which magnified the Lord's power in my heart even more. I was in awe. *How did I get here?* Never would I have thought the Lord would bring me to a leadership conference in Busan, South Korea. It was there I changed how I saw the world I lived in and thought about the rest of the world of which I knew very little. Amidst the different cultures, I saw beauty. I saw eyes being opened, hearts being filled, and Christ being magnified by every nation. As I sat trying to reign in my emotions, my eyes gained clarity. Jesus was captivating my heart all over again and my ambition

131

to follow Him wherever He would lead me. He was showing me there was a destination, and it wasn't only for me. There are thirsty souls everywhere looking for the Living Water that quenches what is dry and dying. My heart was beating with compassion for those who didn't know Christ but also rejoicing for all who did. The new heart I already had in Jesus was waiting to be re-activated and ready to take the next step toward the ultimate destination.

With a new heart comes a new way of living, but so many of us still act like we possess the old heart. Our ways need to change, and our hearts need to open up once again to the revelations God wants us to see. It's time to make that change and remember the ultimate standard we have guiding us.

The Gift Of Righteousness

The second we accepted Jesus, unity was born, and righteousness was declared on us through faith in Him. We died on the cross with our Lord. We became one in sin. We were buried with Him in death. And we were made alive with Him, we were resurrected with Him to newness of life, and we ascended with Him. We are now seated with Him in heavenly places.[92] The imparted gift was perfect, and it cost everything and freely given with no strings attached. What do we do with this? Why does this matter? In Jeremiah 17:7 (NLT), the Bible says, *"But blessed are those who trust in the Lord and have made the Lord their hope and confidence."* Confidence brings us to a place where God's glory becomes the standard by which we want to live. The Bible says:

- ***Through the obedience of Jesus, we have been made righteous—made acceptable to God, and brought into right standing with Him.*** [93]

- ***Jesus made us free, so we are free indeed.*** [94]

- *We are a new creation in Christ.* [95]

- *God is working in us both to desire and do His good pleasure.* [96]

- *We are complete in Him.* [97]

- *We have been blessed with all spiritual blessings in heavenly places in Christ.* [98]

- *We have been raised up with Jesus and now sit with Him in heavenly places.* [99]

- *We can do all things through Christ who strengthens us.* [100]

- *God has not given us a spirit of fear, but a spirit of love, power, and a sound mind.* [101]

- *Because we are believers in Jesus Christ, we can rejoice because our names are written in heaven.* [102]

Once we understand with true confidence who we are in Jesus, everything we do can conform to the highest standard: God's standard. The way we think, feel, and act all play a part. Because we were made alive in Christ, we should now act like we are alive. We no longer rely on godless pleasures to make us happy in the moment, for they are fleeting. Rather, we soak in God's goodness by abounding in thanksgiving. We understand that reflecting God's character and His holiness is the key to a God-powered, fulfilled life. Before we get there, we need to tune our ears to the Word. That's where we recognize how to be led in Godly obedience for Him.

Be Hearers

As I sit and think about reality, especially in 2020, I think *this can't be what I'm seeing and hearing.* The news, the culture, *all of it*, brought on a sense of falling rather than a sense of peace. I want none of that! As a believer, I can take in the same information as everyone else, but I want God's perspective to be the One I act on. Living in this world takes effort, it takes grit, and it takes faith to stick with the Lord until the very end—no matter what. That's why we all need to be hearers of the Word, so we can discern the days ahead, and hold on to the hope that never fails. [103] We don't have to feel as if we are falling into the abyss—discouragement, hardness, brokenness, and dividedness. We can have ears that hear and want to listen with urgency.

In the gospels, the parable of the sower points out four types of ground the Word of God fell on and four ways the Word of God was heard.

- *Luke 8:5 (AMP) says that, first, some seed (some Word) "fell beside the road and it was trampled underfoot, and the birds of the sky ate it up."*

   Then, Luke 8:12 (AMP) interprets, "Those beside the road are the people who have heard; then the devil comes and takes the message [of God] away from their hearts, so that they will not believe [in Me as the Messiah] and be saved."

- *Luke 8:6 (AMP) then says, "Some seed fell on [shallow soil covering] the rocks, and as soon as it sprouted, it withered away, because it had no moisture."*

   Luke 8:13 (AMP) interprets: "Those on the rocky soil are the people who, when they hear, receive and welcome the word with joy; but these have no firmly grounded root. They believe for a while, and in time of trial and temptation they fall away [from Me and abandon their faith]."

- *Next, Luke 8:7 (AMP) says, "Other seed fell among the thorns, and the thorns grew up with it and choked it out."*

  Luke 8:14 (AMP) interprets: "The seed which fell among the thorns, these are the ones who have heard, but as they go on their way they are suffocated with the anxieties and riches and pleasures of this life, and they bring no fruit to maturity."

- *Finally, Luke 8:8 (AMP) says, "And some fell into good soil, and grew up and produced a crop a hundred times as great." As He said these things, He called out, "He who has ears to hear, let him hear and heed My words."*

  And Luke 8:15 (AMP) interprets: "But as for that seed in the good soil, these are the ones who have heard the word with a good and noble heart, and hold on to it tightly, and bear fruit with patience."

From this passage, I would hope and pray all of us have a soil that is good and bearing much fruit. But as we look a smidge further, the key to this parable is found at the end of verse eight. In Luke 8:8 (AMP), Jesus says, *"He who has ears to hear, let him hear and heed My words."* We have to see there are four different kinds of soil mentioned above, not just the one that is good. This means three of the four are not good, and three of the four are not able to accept or keep the Word in their hearts and minds. This alone should spur us to pay attention a little more intently. After all, much of the emphasis is on hearing well.

We live in a world that is decaying, one that doesn't know its right foot from its left—causing many to tune their ears to emptiness. The same is true for some believers. It's our responsibility as followers of Christ to not fall for this emptiness. We *can't* fall for it! Lives are at stake, and Satan and the many distractions of this world are doing everything they can to keep us all from hearing the truth. Satan hates the Word, he hates us, and he doesn't want us to have stability in Christ. He wants us to ignore the Word, think it's too complicated, find it too boring, think it's not accurate, and place it on a shelf to never look at again. I think a lot of us do this and we can't allow this to happen. This is our lifeline being threatened! We have to read our Bible and come with patience knowing Christ will always meet us wherever we are. No matter how hard, how tired, how broken we are, we should never back off God's Word. By hearing, we remember the good and the bad, and we keep meditating, praying, praising and serving the Lord Jesus. This is what being changed from the inside out looks like. The Bible says in Proverbs 4:20–22 (ESV), *"Incline your ear to my sayings. Let them not escape from your sight; keep them within your heart. For they are life to those who find them, and healing to all their flesh. Keep your heart with all vigilance, for from it flow the springs of life."*

Every time we look with undivided affections and lean down to tune our ears to life-giving instructions, we welcome glory. The continual devotion to God's Word opens our senses to comprehension and revelation. This is what changes lives! We all remember when the Lord invaded our hearts. That one verse, one promise, one word, or one person, who stepped up to proclaim the goodness of the Lord. It only takes one revelation to change a life forever. That's why it's so important to remain established in Jesus. When we hear and see with all our hearts, we welcome the opportunity to walk in obedience. In James 1:22–25 (AMP), the Bible says:

> *But prove yourselves doers of the word [actively and con-tinually obeying God's precepts], and not merely listeners [who hear the word but fail to internalize its meaning], deluding yourselves [by unsound reasoning contrary to the truth]. For if anyone only listens to the word without obeying it, he is like a man who looks very carefully at his natural*

face in a mirror; for once he has looked at himself and gone away, he immediately forgets what he looked like. But he who looks carefully into the perfect law, the law of liberty, and faithfully abides by it, not having become a [careless] listener who forgets but an active doer [who obeys], he will be blessed and favored by God in what he does [in his life of obedience].

We actively walk in obedience because we want our lives to display the holiness of God. It's from His holiness that we find what our hearts have been looking for. We need to see the reality of the Bible, and we need to see God for who He is—magnificent! It's time to fight back, to live in order to see and savor Christ fully. Only then will we realize the pleasure we have in knowing Him, and even through disappointments and suffering, our God is in the business of continually making all things new.

The Full Life

"Those were the good old days." I'm sure a lot of us have said this at some point in our lives. The remembered days we want to relive, the ease we walked through, what we thought was the exciting life or the life full of fun and minimal responsibility. The friendships we had, the jobs we loved, and the places we once lived are memories that try to push their way back into existence but can't. The then and now can be a disappointment when all you want to do is escape or go back. I've had this tendency to revert back. When life gets hard or doesn't pan out the way I would like, I want whatever I had in the past. Yet, in the process, I forget all the problems before and in between. I forget the sin that needed to be repented, what I had to go through to get to a certain place, not to mention all the emotions and feelings that tag along. The good old days are nothing more than that: old. I had to change my disposition and remind myself I am never going back.

Jesus helps us look forward with gladness. No longer do we wish for the past. Instead, we remember grace and the gift that was offered—a new heart. Ezekiel 11:19–20 (ESV) says, *"And I will give them one heart, and a new spirit I will put within them. I will remove the heart of stone from their flesh and give them a heart of flesh, that they may walk in my statutes and keep my rules and obey them. And they shall be my people, and I will be their God."* It's not only about receiving a new heart but allowing that heart to be transformed into the image of Christ. In 1 Peter 1:16 (AMP), it says, *"Because it is written, 'You shall be holy (set apart), for I am holy.'"* A new heart, once dead to the things of God, can now operate under the Holy Spirit as it was intended. Our hearts need to become responsive to the One who makes us holy. We need holiness.

Holiness is one of the most glorious words in the Bible, even if it can seem unreachable. We may feel a little arrogant to think we could obtain it, or perhaps the Bible seems too boring, causing us not to think about it at all. I find myself thinking about what it means to be holy and sometimes all I can think is, *there's no way I can live that way all the time. I mean, what about all the debris in my heart and all the battles smashing around me? How is holiness going to help me be triumphant?*

David knew that when we finally come to know the place where God's instruction lies in our hearts, then the highways of Zion become visible, taking us to where we need to be.[104] He knew that triumph doesn't just come at the end of a battle but also at the beginning or even during. When we look to the Word of God, that's where we find rest, peace, and the strength we need to get through any trial. By lifting up our praise and standing on the promises of God, this is where victory comes, and holiness takes root. The roots of godliness and holiness can honestly be quite painful as we wrestle with tragedy, trials, and persecution that won't leave our hearts. This is exactly when we should long for the things of God the most. The process of holiness doesn't mean we won't go through the disappointments or sufferings in life. It means we can have joy in the midst of the battles. Joy comes when we receive inner strength from the Lord, and when we treasure Him the most. Isaiah 33:6 (AMP) says, *"And He will be the security and stability of your times, a treasure of salvation, wisdom and knowledge; The fear of the Lord is your treasure."*

The Lord wants us all to know that we can be intentional people who want to live an upright life. In 2 Corinthians 7:1 (AMP) the Bible says, *"Therefore, since we have these [great and wonderful] promises, beloved, let us cleanse ourselves from everything that contaminates body and spirit, completing holiness [living a consecrated life—a life set apart for God's purpose] in the fear of God."* We've had to fight this far in life and along the way hopefully have found confidence in the fact that goodness is coming. One day, we will be utterly free and, our lifelong battles and the kingdom of death and darkness will forever be destroyed.[105] Until then, we stand firm waiting for that promise. We lift our eyes to the hills and see our help. The maker of the heavens and the earth is right here with us.[106]

An established heart knows what gift it has been given and acknowledges that the new heart wasn't meant to lay dormant. It was meant to be set apart for God's purpose to be led by the Holy Spirit and to love God and others. In 1 Thessalonians 3:13 (ESV), the Bible says,

> *"Now may our God and Father himself, and our Lord Jesus, direct our way to you, and may the Lord make you increase and abound in love for one another and for all, as we do for you, so that he may establish your hearts blameless in holiness before our God and Father, at the coming of our Lord Jesus with all his saints."*

The invisible fight, although cluttered at times, has the ability, in Christ, to break through the darkness. Psalm 36:9 (AMP) says, *"For with You is the fountain of life [the fountain of life-giving water]; In Your light we see light."* To have a God-powered, fulfilling life, we need true transformation that not only breaks through the debris but sees the glory of Jesus and wants to live that out continuously.

I leave you with this verse from Ephesians 3:14-21 (NLT):

When I think of all this, I fall to my knees and pray to the Father, the Creator of everything in heaven and on earth. I pray that from his glorious, unlimited resources he will empower you with inner strength through his Spirit. Then Christ will make his home in your hearts as you trust in him. Your roots will grow down into God's love and keep you strong. And may you have the power to understand, as all God's people should, how wide, how long, how high, and how deep his love is. May you experience the love of Christ, though it is too great to understand fully. Then you will be made complete with all the fullness of life and power that comes from God. Now all glory to God, who is able, through his mighty power at work within us, to accomplish infinitely more than we might ask or think. Glory to him in the church and in Christ Jesus through all generations forever and ever! Amen.

Amen and Amen!

Part Three
Reflections for the Heart
Chapters 11 & 12

Review: We have seen what reality has been, currently is, and can be in the future. The Word of God needs to be our reality. It can't just be another book we place on a shelf, forgotten and unread. This is our lifeline and needs to be guarded at all times. The enemy is out to destroy us, but the Promise Maker never fails, and His Word never returns void. He remains faithful from beginning to end. It's time for light to shine in the dark places of our hearts and for breakthroughs to happen. As truth begins to penetrate deep within, it leaves hope for the weary and strength for the weak. Our affections change when we live the God-powered life we were meant to have.

Final thoughts: God's holiness should not only take our breath away but cause us to be set apart on purpose and for a purpose. Because He is Holy, we are called to be holy. It's not a process that gains perfection but one that discovers how the hidden battlegrounds shape us to be more like Jesus. We keep moving forward, keep fighting the good fight, and we see this life for what it is. We know that we are but a vapor just passing through, and as we wait for heaven, we never lose sight of the privilege, like Ephesians 5:2 (ESV) says, to *"walk in love, as Christ loved us and gave himself up for us, a fragrant offering and sacrifice to God."* We are the aroma of Christ to God and to others. Psalm 29:2 (ESV) says, *"Ascribe to the LORD the glory due his name; worship the LORD in the splendor of holiness."*

Discussion Questions and Prayers

- **Can God ever soften our calloused heart?** Think this through and ask the Lord to reveal anything that might be turning your heart a little too hard toward life, God, and others.

  _____

  _____

  o Lord, we know that in You, a heart can be transformed from stone to flesh in an instant. We understand how easily hardness can emerge; therefore we pray for hearts that never want to miss out on what you want to teach. We will not grow hard, but remain meek and tender, allowing the Holy Spirit to guide in whatever direction is best.

- **Is our divided heart getting harder to spot?** Ask the Lord to reveal anything you aren't willing to give up to follow him completely.

  _____

  _____

  o Lord, we pray you help us fight against the debris clouding our minds and hearts. We pray for wholeness in you, not half-hearted devotion that can quickly vanish, as the world gains access to our emotions and desires. When illusions tempt us to take one step away from Jesus, I pray we stop and run to the foot of the cross instead. Thank you for Your armor we can put on daily to help fight against Satan's many darts.

- **Can anyone understand our broken heart?** Ask the Lord to heal what is broken and to give you an unyielding determination to rise again.

  _____

  _____

  o Lord, we know that no one will ever understand the depths of our brokenness, but you do! Lord, you are near and know exactly how we feel because You lived it. You took the very punishment we all deserved and willingly walked to the cross with all Your heart. We thank you for life, and in the midst of pain, thank you for reminding us of your goodness and mercy. It's with those precious gifts that we gain the opportunity to help others.

- **Will our fearful heart ever be free?** Take your fears to the Lord and ask for His perfect peace to cover you.

  _____

  _____

  o Lord, we thank you for our freedom in You. We remember with confidence, fear has no hold on us when we seek the One who brings perfect peace. We have the ability to not fear, but when it does spring up, when our peace is in jeopardy, we remember You are the author and finisher of our faith.

- **Has our discouraged heart finally gone numb?** Go back to the basics and thank the Lord for all He has done.

  _____

  _____

  o Lord, we pray that discouragement turns into encouragement. As we cling to the hope You bring, we continually give back, even when we start to grow faint. We don't give up. Instead, we take heart. We remember that we aren't alone and forgotten. The moments we don't understand are when God is training us up to be champions for Him.

- **Can we beat carnality and have transformation that is effective?** Allow His mercy to move you to repentance, and ask the Lord for strength in your weakness.

  _____

  _____

  o Lord, we thank you for calling us out, for correcting and disciplining us when needed. We have a God that truly cares, who wants the best for us. Lord, help us to not sway, help us to keep one foot in front of the other with obedience. Lord, when we do veer off track, when we do become distracted and disillusioned, we thank you for Your faithfulness and for 1 John 1:9. You always make a way for us to come back. We remember it's not in shame and guilt that we come but with a heart willing to stand boldly at the throne of grace.

- **Are soft hearts coming from intentional living?** Thank the Lord for people and ask Him to give you a heart that loves them as He does.

  _____

  _____

  - Lord, we pray against division and call for unity. Help us take responsibility with our intentionality toward others. Give us hearts that yearn to speak life and show your love abundantly. The only way to see and love people the way we should is to love You first. We thank You for leaving us an example on how to love and pray we can start to master this today.

- **Are we true worshippers?** Ask the Lord for a yearning to be in His presence. Thank Him for having the opportunity to seek His face.

  _____

  _____

  - Lord, we thank you that intimacy with you can happen anytime, anywhere, and any day. We pray we never lose our wonderment of You as we develop into worshippers that know their rightful place. Thank you for rescuing us from our own moments of glory and allowing us to go deeper still in Your presence.

- **Can we live redeemed with eyes lifted to eternity?** Eternity will be here soon, but until then, thank the Lord for that promise. Keep imagining with deep joy and anticipation what it will be like.

  _____

  _____

  - Lord, we thank you for making a way when there was no way. Help us to see you with the eyes of our hearts. We long, not for things of this world, but for the joy set before us. Like you, we lift our eyes to keep the battles we face in perspective. Yes, we have so much to look forward to, but as we wait, we focus on shining the light of Christ to those around us now.

- **Will You ignite our passionate hearts for You?** Pray for a desire to share Christ's love no matter the cost.

  _____

  _____

  - Lord, thank you for the gift of life as we remember to count our days. Help us to remember Your greatness and the point of the Christian life. We pray for urgency—we pray for hearts passionate for reading the Word, prayer, and fasting. As we come to understand the gifts you have given us, may we use it all for Your glory. We thank you for the privilege to be part of Your story, and we know that until our hearts stop beating, we still have purpose.

- **Is holiness something we desire?** Ask the Lord to re-activate your heart and to show you His love in a whole new way.

  _____

  _____

  - Lord, thank you for our new hearts and for the gift of righteousness. It cost everything yet was freely given because You loved us that much. We pray for confidence in Who you say we are and live in a way so others see Your glory. Lord, we ask that holiness take root in our hearts and allows us to live a God-powered life that finds fulfillment completely in Jesus.

Notes

Introduction:

1. Isaiah 40:8

2. Bloom, Jon, Story. In *Don't Follow Your Heart: God's Ways Are Not Your Ways,* p.7. Minneapolis, MN: Desiring God, 2015.

3. "KJV Dictionary Definition: Establish." AV1611.com. Accessed September 17, 2020. https://av1611.com/kjbp/kjv-dictionary/establish.html.

Chapter 1:

4. Mark 6: 45–52

5. Romans 8:28

Chapter 2:

6. Robinson, Robert. *"Come Thou Fount of Every Blessing,"* 1758.

7. Reinke, Tony. Story. In *Competing Spectacles: Treasuring Christ in the Media Age*, p.143. Wheaton, IL: Crossway, 2019.

8. Reinke, Tony. Story. In *Competing Spectacles: Treasuring Christ in the Media Age*, p.144. Wheaton, IL: Crossway, 2019.

9. 1 Corinthians 6:12

10. Luke 15:11-32

Chapter 3:

11. Spurgeon, Charles H. "Christ's Hospital." C.H. Spurgeon: Spurgeon's Sermons Volume 38: 1892- Christian Classics Ethereal Library, June 12, 1892. https://www.ccel.org/ccel/spurgeon/sermons38.xxiv.html.

12. John 16:33

13. Romans 8:28

14. Lucado, Max. Story. In *You'll Get Through This: Hope And Help for Your Turbulent Times*, p.83. Nashville, TN: Thomas Nelson, 2013.

15. Hebrews 13:5

16. Genesis 39:7

17. 1 Peter 5:8-10

18. Romans 16:20

19. Proverbs 24:16

Chapter 4:

20. Genesis 12:10-20, Genesis 16, Genesis 20:1-16

21. Numbers 13-14

22. "Romans 1 Matthew Henry's Commentary." Accessed February 8, 2020. https://biblehub.com/commentaries/mhc/romans/1.htm.

23. "KJV Dictionary Definition: Dismay." AV1611.com. Accessed September 10, 2020. http://av1611.com/kjbp/kjv-dictionary/dismay.html.

24. John 20:19

25. Matthew 28:5, John 20:19

26. Hebrews 12:2

27. Hebrews 4:1

28. Exodus 14:13-16

29. Psalm 55:22

Chapter 5:

30. Matthew 7: 24-25

31. Psalm 90:2

32. Psalm 18:2

33. Ecclesiastes 8:17

34. Matthew 11:3, Luke 7:19

35. Walvoord, John F., and Roy B. Zuck. Essay. In *The Bible Knowledge Commentary. An Exposition of the Scriptures*, p.43. Wheaton, IL: SP Publications, INC, 1983.

36. Hebrews 4:12

37. *Ain't Nobody Got Time For That (Original + AutoTune)*. NobodyGotTimeForThis, 2013. https://www.youtube.com/watch?v=waEC-8GFTP4.

38. 1 Samuel 1:11

39. Sumrall, Lester. Introduction. In *The Making of a Champion*, p.9. New Kensington, PA: Whitaker House, 1995.

40. Nehemiah 1:1-11

41. John 14:13

42. John 5:19

43. John 15:5

44. Psalm 23:3

Chapter 6:

45. Acts 9

46. Matthew 20:19, Mark 10:34, and Luke 18:32; Isaiah 52:14

47. Matthew 21:42, Acts 4:11 and Mark 12:10

48. Matthew 27:35-37

49. Galatians 1:4

50. Isaiah 43:19

51. 1 Corinthians 6:19

52. Acts 2

53. "Carnal." Dictionary.com. Dictionary.com. Accessed September 17, 2020. http://www.dictionary.com/browse/carnality.

54. Isaiah 14:13

55. John 14:27

56. Proverbs 3:5-6

Chapter 7:

57. Proverbs 16:18, Proverbs 29:23

58. 1 John 1:9

59. 2 Thessalonians 1:3

60. Luke 10:25-37

61. Ephesians 2:8

Chapter 8:

62. Isaiah 43:7, Isaiah 43:21

63. John 15:15

64. 2 Corinthians 2:15

65. Piper, John. "God Is Most Glorified in Us When We Are Most Satisfied in Him," *Desiring God*, October 13, 2012. https://www.desiringgod.org/messages/god-is-most-glorified-in-us-when-we-are-most-satisfied-in-him.

66. Murray, Andrew Said, DD. *Waiting on God* (Northern Ireland and South Carolina: Ambassador, 1997), pp.88-89. Quoted in M. Redman, *Facedown* (Ventura, CA: Regal Books, 2004), 81.

67. Tozer A.W. Said, *Heights of Delight* (Ventura, CA: Regal Books, 2002), n.p. Quoted in M. Redman, *Facedown* (Ventura, CA: Regal Books, 2004), 80.

68. Psalm 73:26

Chapter 9:

69. 1 Corinthians 6:20

70. Psalm 103:4

71. Psalm 36:5-6

72. Revelation 7:13-17, Revelation 21:4-8,Revelation 22:3-7, Revelation 22:5

73. 2 Peter 3:13

74. Safwat, Kerolos. Facebook, 2019. https://www. facebook.com/photo.php?fbid=10214346481037218 &set=pb.1272960198.-2207520000..&type=3

75. Colossians 3:4, Romans 8:30, 2 Corinthians 4:17, Galatians 5:5, 1 Peter 5:10

76. John 21:7

Chapter 10:

77. 1 Corinthians 9:27

78. Ephesians 1:18

79. Matthew 5:15

80. Strong's Greek: 2564. καλέω (kaleó) -- to call. Accessed August 22, 2020. https://biblehub.com/greek/2564.htm.

81. "A Quote by Mother Teresa." Goodreads. Goodreads. Accessed August 22, 2020. https://www.goodreads.com/quotes/55807-i-do-not-pray-for-success-i-ask-for-faithfulness.

82. Hyatt, Michael S., and Daniel Harkavy. "Chapter 4." Essay. In *Living Forward: a Proven Plan to Stop Drifting and Get the Life You Want*, 61–85. Grand Rapids, MI, MI: Baker Books, a division of Baker Publishing Group, 2016.

83. Matthew 24:36, Mark 13:32

84. John 17:4

85. John 3:30

Chapter 11:

86. Spurgeon, C. H., and Alistair Begg. "January 9." Essay. In *Morning and Evening Daily Devotions*, p.48. Wheaton, IL: Crossway, 2003.

87. Proverbs 13:4

88. Exodus 17:15, Psalm 20:5

89. Numbers 23:19

90. Mark 4:38-40

91. John 21:18

Chapter 12:

92. Romans 6:4-11, Ephesians 2:5–6

93. Romans 5:19

94. John 8:36

95. 2 Corinthians 5:17

96. Philippians 2:13

97. Colossians 2:10

98. Ephesians 1:3

99. Ephesians 2:6

100. Philippians 4:13

101. 2 Timothy 1:7

102. Luke 10:20

103. Philippians 1:9-10

104. Psalm 84:5

105. Colossians 1:13

106. Psalm 121

About the Author

Jacky Elwood is a wife to Jason and mother to two sons, Jameson and Jack. After earning a business marketing degree from George Mason University, God put it on Jacky's heart to write. She feels it's important to be obedient to whatever task God gives you, however big or small. Encouraging women through God's Word and her own life experiences is not only her calling but also her passion.

Connect with Jacky at: JackyElwood.com or on social media @Jackyelwood